Accessing Your Inner Secrets

Mastering the Art of Emotional Wellness With Empowered Tapping®

Leonie Blackwell

A self-published title
Animal Dreaming Publishing
www.AnimalDreamingPublishing.com

Accessing Your Inner Secrets

A self-published book produced with the help and support of
Animal Dreaming Publishing
PO Box 672
Samford Village
QLD 4520
Australia

publish@animaldreamingpublishing.com
AnimalDreamingPublishing.com
@animaldreamingpublishing
@AnimalDreamingPublishing

First published in 2024

leonie@bwellinstitute.com
leonieblackwell.au
@empoweredtapping

A catalogue record for this publication is available from the National Library of Australia.

ISBN 978-1-7637448-0-6

The information in this book is intended for spiritual and emotional guidance only. It is not intended to replace medical advice or treatment.

To You, My Inspiration.

Contents

Introduction **9**

The Need-Fear Cycle and Trauma 9

What Tapping Can Do For You 12

How to Tap 15

The Tapping Experience 18

How to Use This Book 19

Cycles **21**

Cycle 1. Love/Abandonment 22

Cycle 2. Belonging/Aloneness 25

Cycle 3. Acceptance/Rejection 28

Cycle 4. Approval/Inferiority 31

Cycle 5. Worthy/Undeserving 34

Cycle 6. Okay/Being Wrong 38

Cycle 7. Valued/Invisible 42

Cycle 8. Equal/Innate Deficit 45

Cycle 9. Needed/Unloved 49

Cycle 10. Safe/Violated 52

Cycle 11. Existing/Unwanted 56

Cycle 12. Competent/Inadequate 59

Cycle 13. Dignity/Faulty 62

Cycle 14. Protected/Powerless 66

Cycle 15. Security/Lack 70
Cycle 16. Significance/Insignificance 74
Cycle 17. Honesty/Deception 78
Cycle 18. Respected/Overlooked 82
Cycle 19. Nurtured/Attention Withheld 86
Cycle 20. Supported/Vulnerable 90
Cycle 21. Important/Ignored 94
Cycle 22. Trust/Betrayal 97
Cycle 23. Understood/Compassion Withheld 101
Cycle 24. Connected/Disconnected 105
Cycle 25. Authentic/Imperfection 109
Cycle 26. Adored/Care Withheld 113
Cycle 27. Special/Love Withheld 117
Cycle 28. Admired/Interest Withheld 121
Cycle 29. Cherished/Empathy Withheld 124
Cycle 30. Reward and Celebration/Punishment 128
Cycle 31. Innocence/Blamed 132
Cycle 32. Enough/Judged 136
Cycle 33. Sensual/Undesired 140
Cycle 34. Integrity/Betraying Your Moral Conscience 143
Cycle 35. Sacred Sexual Connection/Loneliness 147
Cycle 36. Belonging with Like-Minded Souls/The Guilt of Not Belonging 150
Cycle 37. Purpose/Pointlessness 154
Cycle 38. Whole/Disintegration 157
Cycle 39. Free and Independent/Trapped 160
Cycle 40. Shining Brightly/Dulled 164

Empowered Realisms **169**
Empowered Realism 1. Your Beliefs Are Always Right 170
Empowered Realism 2. To Every Rule An Exception 173
Empowered Realism 3. Sometimes It's About You, Sometimes It's Not 176
Empowered Realism 4. BIG-You and Small-You 179
Empowered Realism 5. It's All Just Data: Information You Can Utilise 182
Empowered Realism 6. Proportional Response 185
Empowered Realism 7. Your Experiences Don't Make You Who You Are 188

Emotional Continuums **191**
The Anger Continuum 192
The Fear Continuum 192
The Shame Continuum 192
The Jealousy Continuum 193
The Guilt Continuum 193
The Grief Continuum 193
The Depression Continuum 193
The Trauma Continuum 193
The Powerlessness Continuum 194
The Sabotage Continuum 194

Acknowledgements **197**

About the Author **199**

Introduction

Over the millennia of human existence, our ability to feel has consistently prevailed. Remarkably, this innate aspect of our nature has continued to be misunderstood and subjected to suppression, shame, denial and scrutiny. Our ability to feel has encountered punishment, blame and projection, which ultimately contributed to the eruption of emotional discord within society. Perhaps due to this tumultuous journey, we find ourselves no closer to mastering the effective management of our emotions. It's high time for a change.

Empowered Tapping® is a catalyst for emotional transformation. This book will be your guide, leading you through a process of healing to address the consequences of centuries of inadequate emotional management.

Make the most of this journey by first learning to recognise the driving forces behind your emotional responses. Next, delve into the underlying ideas shaping your interpretations. Finally, expand your emotional vocabulary so you can articulate your feelings more accurately. With these foundations laid, the key to rewiring your brain's neural pathways and fostering new and authentic ways of thinking lies in Empowered Tapping®. Join me on this exploration of emotional wellness as we access the inner secrets embedded in the Need-Fear Cycle. These treasures pave the path for a profound shift in how we understand and navigate the intricate terrain of our emotions.

The Need-Fear Cycle and Trauma

In the intricate dance of human emotions, the Need-Fear Cycle unveils itself as a recurring pattern with profound implications. Picture this: a need arises, and unmet, it triggers an unsettling fear about your identity. Physically, this fear manifests as anxiety and nervousness, creating an undeniable discomfort. Your cognitive response is a quest for relief, leading your mind to search for a solution. Embarking on the quest to fulfil your need brings some satisfaction. However, months may pass, and when the need remains unmet, the cycle renews. As this pattern repeats, fear intensifies, discomfort heightens, and your mind, seemingly unaware of the cycle, seeks solace in the familiar — the unmet need.

Each return to the unmet need feels like a fresh revelation with a potential solution that holds a glimmer of hope for a better future. Yet, it's a continuation of the same cycle, which can persist over years and leave you in a state of perpetual discontent.

In essence, the Need-Fear Cycle manifests as a relentless pattern of dissatisfaction. The repeating loop that weaves through the fabric of our lives can be summarised in four pivotal steps:

1. You have an unmet need.
2. You fear what it says about you.
3. Your mind actively seeks a solution.
4. Time is invested in pursuing the fulfilment of the need.

The more cycles you navigate, the more profound the pain becomes. This accumulation of emotional turmoil creates miniature trauma responses to everyday experiences. Each unmet need triggers a trauma response, which becomes intertwined with the fear that serves as its expression.

Continued entanglement in this cycle can lead to an emotional landscape akin to post-traumatic stress syndrome despite the absence of war or life-threatening events. Your limbic system, particularly the amygdala, then interprets experiences as threats to your identity, self-expression and ego.

Over time, unmet needs and their associated fears gradually accumulate and stifle your authentic self. However, there is a way out. The Empowered Tapping® shared in this book serves as a key to unlocking the Need-Fear-Trauma Cycle.

By liberating you from its grip, it empowers you to live authentically and embrace the life you genuinely desire.

Understanding the Three Triggers of Your Reactions

Recognising the factors that shape your interactions and interpretations of events throughout the recovery journey is crucial. The three key factors are:

1. How others treat you.
2. How you treat yourself.
3. How you treat others.

In simple terms, how you are treated often becomes internalised, influencing how you treat yourself and, subsequently, how you interact with others. The treatment you receive during your formative years forms the unconscious data that filters all subsequent experiences.

The events during your teenage years solidify, dissolve or create new interpretations of your identity and expectations of how you should be treated.

As you carry this varied and complex array of experiences into adulthood, your memories significantly contribute to how others treat you, how you treat yourself and how you treat the people in your life.

Observable Patterns in Relationships

You can often observe these dynamics in your relationships by noticing:

- the way people treat you is influenced by how you allow them to treat you.
- the way people treat you is influenced by how you are accustomed to being treated.
- the way people treat you is influenced by how you treat yourself.

Self-Perception and Behaviour

Your self-concept, the picture you've created of yourself, determines how you respond to others and the way you treat yourself. Once you've formed a picture of your world within yourself, your self-perception colours every experience and influences how others perceive you.

The Impact of Self-Belief

When you don't allow others to treat you well, you unintentionally teach them to treat you with disrespect. This negative spiral can lead to a self-fulfilling prophecy, where your view of yourself is continually validated. The more you reinforce your negative self-perception, the more others may interact with you in negative ways, further cementing the cycle.

Breaking the Cycle

Being your best possible self within the Need-Fear Cycle is undoubtedly challenging. Recognising and understanding your triggers is the first step in establishing new patterning. By fostering positive self-perception and setting boundaries that align with self-respect, you can reshape your interactions with others and cultivate a healthier, more positive reality for yourself.

Empowered Tapping®

Empowered Tapping® is a scripted conversation with parts of your brain. This conversation specifically unlocks the repeating patterns in your emotional, cognitive and physical lives and rewires your brain. The specific words in the scripts do all the work of undoing the emotional and cognitive stories (patterns) running in your limbic system for you. By marking the neural pathway to be dissolved during sleep, they pave the way for permanent and rewarding change. Tapping is the process of rhythmically tapping specific meridian points with your fingertips. Empowered Tapping® combines the benefits of tapping with a specific set of words to release the addictive patterns that lock you into trauma responses. It is powerful and life-changing.

What Tapping Can Do For You

Tapping on meridian points creates change in the body in four ways. It influences:

1. The meridian system.
2. The biochemistry of the body.
3. Gene expression.
4. The rewiring of neural pathways.

The Meridian System

Research has been conducted on how tapping on meridian points resolves emotional distress. It has been shown to be one of the most effective techniques available. Stimulating a meridian point moves the Chi or energy in the meridian, unblocking it and returning flow to the body. The Chinese believe the first indication of an energy block or imbalance is a change in emotional expression, mood or cognitive response. When the block is not removed or cleared, the symptoms progress and are expressed as physical symptoms like headaches. If the symptoms are not resolved, they develop into illness and disease. Thus, learning to manage your emotions effectively can prevent illness, disease and general symptoms of malaise.

The Biochemistry of the Body

Discussing the fight-flight-freeze response and the hormones involved is all the rage — and there is a good reason why. Cortisol, the adrenal hormone released in response to stress, sustains the heightened state of stress.

Here's what you need to know:

- The body releases adrenaline in response to any stressor.
- Adrenaline prepares you to fight the threat or run like crazy from it.
- Adrenaline moves blood away from the brain and digestive system and into the muscles and heart.
- Adrenaline is the primary hormone released during the first twenty minutes of stress, during which time the perceived immediate danger can be addressed. The adrenal glands can then stop releasing adrenaline.
- Nor-adrenaline can then be secreted to return the body to balance – back to a state of calm.
- The effects of adrenaline can last up to one hour.
- When a perceived threat persists beyond twenty minutes, cortisol is released from the cortex of the adrenal glands. This is common with cognitive or emotional triggers, where the threat is perceived as ongoing.
- Initially, cortisol helps you survive whatever is going on. But when it is continuously released, the effects become negative. The body is only meant to be in a stress state for short periods.

- Cortisol shuts down your ability to remember things. It supports degenerative processes in the body and compromises your immune function. Having cortisol surge through your body for extended periods is simply not good for you. Under normal circumstances, cortisol is at its highest level in your body in the morning — around 5 a.m. It then slowly decreases over the day to be at its lowest level in the evening.
- When traumatised or chronically stressed, cortisol levels remain high throughout the day. Some may even have cortisol levels that are reversed — low in the morning and high in the evening.
- Tapping on meridian points lowers cortisol levels by twenty-four per cent, thereby reducing stress levels.

Gene Expression

David Feldstein and Dawson Church researched how tapping switches off the gene for PTSD. The research demonstrated that tapping facilitates short and long-term changes in the way the brain and body respond to triggers and that gene expression was altered by tapping. This research proved that tapping works.

The gene for PTSD is the fastest to be activated, which is why someone can be fine one second and trembling, hyperventilating, shaking, confused or panicked the next. But it can also be switched off just as quickly, and tapping does that. This means tapping can help switch off the gene while lowering the cortisol levels and assisting the body's energy flow.

Rewiring Neural Pathways

In the past, it was considered that once the neural pathways in the brain formed, they were set and immovable. The term plasticity is now commonplace in conversations about the brain. It means that the brain forms, dissolves and re-makes its neural pathways. We may, in fact, be able to teach an old dog new tricks! Synaptic pruning is the process of unlearning patterns.

Glial cells are known as the gardeners of our brains. Some can speed up communication between nerve cells, while others digest neural cells that are no longer in use. The ones that do the gardening are called microglial cells. These are the ones involved in pruning our synaptic connections.

When using the Empowered Tapping® scripts, there is an immediate shift in how you feel. This shift continues to resolve the stress associated with the issue you are addressing for hours following the tapping. The next day, after sleep, there is a sense of newness or transformation that comes with the sensation that this is how you always felt. It is as if the you from yesterday is a distant memory. Combining tapping with the Empowered Tapping® scripts ensures that a neural pathway is unplugged and reformed to create a new and healthy connection. At this point, the body marks the old synapse with proteins that the microglial cells detect, bond to and destroy while you sleep. You then wake up refreshed and functioning in your new reality.

How to Tap

Use your pointer and middle fingers to tap on the meridian points indicated on the diagram. Tap five to seven times on each point while saying the words in the script for that point. The tapping action is firm enough to create a rhythmic vibration but not so hard that it feels like you are trying to hurt the body. When tapping a specific script, tap all rounds in the script in sequence. To complete a script, tap from round one until the final empowering round. You can tap a script more than once. Tapping the same script for three days in a row is often helpful. You can also tap two or three scripts per day. You will know when you have had enough tapping because you will feel tired as if you've had enough. After tapping, it is always advisable to drink a glass of water. If you feel tired, go for a quick walk in the fresh air for five to ten minutes to recalibrate your energy.

The Order of Tapping

The Empowered Tapping® scripts include letters that indicate which point to tap while saying the correlating text. Begin each process at the top of your head (TH) and proceed in order to conclude at the points under the arms (UA).

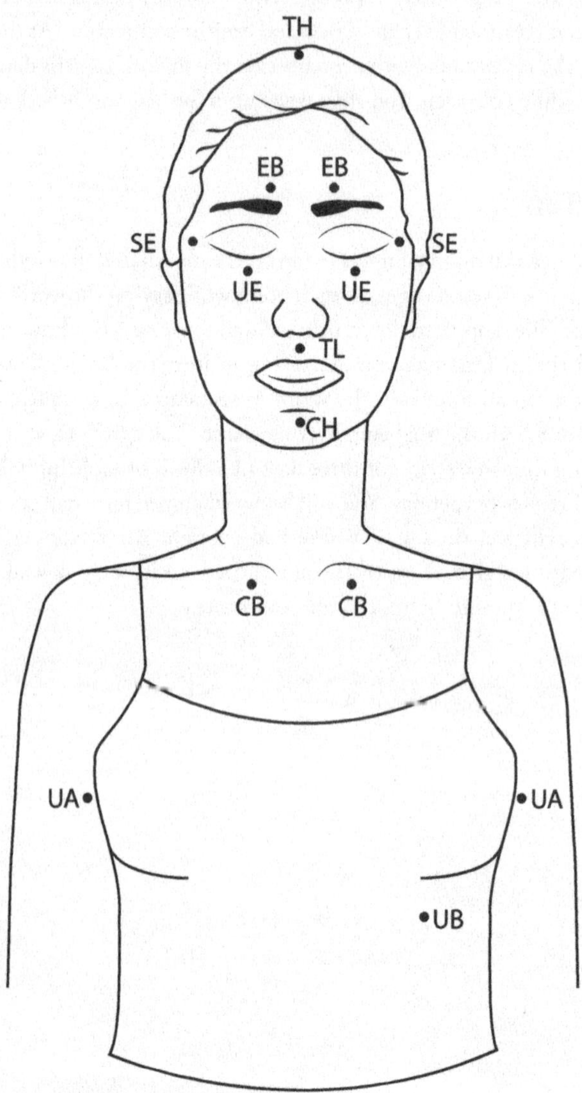

The order is:

1. Top of Head (TH)
2. Eyebrows (EB)
3. Side of Eyes (SE)
4. Under Eyes (UE)
5. Top of Lip (TL)
6. Chin (CH)
7. Collarbones (CB)
8. Under the Breast on the right-hand side (UB)
9. Under the Arms (UA)

Each point represents an emotional or cognitive vibration, which explains why one point can be sore when others aren't. By understanding the emotion or thought process related to each meridian point, you can gain a greater understanding of your emotional reactions and cognitive beliefs surrounding the events in your life.

When a point becomes blocked, it creates an imbalance in expression. Once the blockage is cleared, the point can be tapped to assist in the expression of life-affirming thoughts and feelings.

The Top of the Head (TH): Tap this point to clear blocks around integrating experiences and feelings into learnt lessons. Once cleared, tapping facilitates greater confidence.

The Eyebrows (EB): Tapping the points above each eyebrow clears inflexibility created by shock and terror. This blockage leads to the fear of futility. Once cleared, tapping these points facilitates hope, calmness and a sense of peace.

The Side of the Eyes (SE): Tapping the side of the eyes clears indecision and the feeling of being discouraged by life. Once cleared, tapping these points facilitates courage, tolerance and the ability to take initiative.

Under the Eyes (UE): Tap these points to clear obsessive worry, scepticism, mistrust and suspicion. Once cleared, tapping under the eyes facilitates a sense of fairness, openness, caring and trust.

The Top of Lip (TL): Tap here to clear self-doubt that stems from the unmet need for love and support. Once cleared, tapping this point facilitates self-consciousness and the capacity to have needs met and feel supported.

The Chin (CH): Tapping the chin clears the sense of being overwhelmed and feelings of vulnerability and being stuck. It also removes blockages that have you holding on to a current reality when it is no longer sustainable. Once cleared, tapping this point facilitates the capacity to revitalise and reinvigorate flow and to feel centred and secure within.

The Collarbone (CB): Tap these points to clear hysteria, paranoia, fear, nervousness, anxiety and insecurity. Once cleared, tapping the collarbone points facilitates rationality, clear perception, self-understanding and gentleness.

Under the Breast (UB): Tapping this point under the right breast clears frustration, anger, rage, irritability, resentment, jealousy and guilt. Once cleared, tapping here facilitates kindness, compassion and generosity.

Under the Arms (UA): Tap under either arm point or, if you are able, under both arms simultaneously to clear rejection, addiction, attachment, self-pity and clouded thinking. Once cleared, tapping here facilitates self-acceptance, fairness, openness and deep thinking.

The Tapping Experience

If you have never tapped before, it helps to know what to expect. It is entirely normal, in fact pretty exciting, when you yawn, burp or sneeze while saying the words in the tapping scripts. These responses are a sign that energy is being released. Sometimes, when issues are significant, your amygdala will resist their release. When this happens, you will feel really tired, like you can't even speak, during the tapping. If you can, keep going. If not, stop for the moment and return to your tapping process the next day. Afterwards, you may feel tired or thirsty. Drink plenty of water and get on with your typical day. Shifts will continue throughout the day. Once you have slept, you will wake up feeling renewed.

Before you launch into the body of the book, note that the wording of the tapping scripts is intentional. You may wonder about the scripts' unconventional grammar, and the statements may sound a little awkward when read out loud. However, every word has a purpose and a reason the scripts have been written as they are. When you start tapping the sentences, the order of words makes sense inside your head, and they work on your limbic system to create change. Changing the grammar would lessen the impact of the process. You will know the scripts are doing their job when your mind disagrees with what you are saying or when you yawn, burp, stumble over the words or feel tired. These are all signs that the process is working, and it's exciting.

How to Use This Book

This transformative guide on emotional well-being is organised into three distinct sections: Cycles, Empowered Realism and Emotional Continuums. Each section features Empowered Tapping® scripts for you to use.

Each of the forty cycle scripts begins with a detailed description to illustrate how the Need-Fear Cycle may be triggered by others' actions, self-treatment or your perceptions. Following this, reflective journal prompts encourage a deeper exploration of your personal experiences. Finally, there is the tapping script, which you can engage to release emotional tension.

The seven Empowered Realism philosophies are explained and accompanied by journal prompts to help you understand their implications. The Empowered Tapping® scripts in this section are designed to peel away layers of limiting beliefs. In the Emotional Continuums section, you will discover a versatile template for addressing specific emotions and clearing their charges.

There's no prescribed order for working through the tapping scripts. You can start from the beginning and progress sequentially or follow your intuition, selecting topics that resonate with you. Alternatively, open the book to any page and tap the script you encounter. Tailor your selection by tapping scripts that align with your current emotions and challenges. The potential of empowered change lies in your willingness to initiate the tapping process — your brain won't rewire itself without your active engagement.

As a bonus, I have recorded a couple of additional tapping scripts for you. They can be found at www.leonieblackwell.au/accessingyourinnersecrets

Cycles

This section contains forty cycle scripts, each addressing an unmet need. For a comprehensive approach, you might like to work through each cycle in order. This can be helpful as we are rarely conscious of our conditioning. By their very nature, unmet needs can be hidden drivers. You can also scan the chapter headings and choose the cycles you are drawn to, either following your instinct or addressing an area relevant to your present scenarios.

Each Need-Fear Cycle is introduced with information on how it may present in your day-to-day encounters. It may be triggered by others' actions, self-treatment or your perceptions. Before jumping into the tapping scripts, take a moment to reflect on the journal prompts. Writing down your responses will encourage a deeper exploration of your personal experiences. Prepare for your tapping experience by sitting, standing or lying in a comfortable position in a quiet space where you will not be disturbed. The scripts take about five minutes to run through. You may like to put fifteen to twenty minutes aside so you can complete the session without feeling rushed or being interrupted.

It is helpful to note the unconventional structure of the tapping scripts. Some of the phrasing may sound awkward and be grammatically incorrect. You may catch your mind wanting to swap words around. Be mindful that the order of the words is very intentional. When you tap on the meridian points and say the sentences, they will make sense to your brain and do the work they are designed to do. While I'm always excited to know we have engaged your brain and got its attention, reading the words in the script as they are written is important to your healing process.

Cycle 1. Love/Abandonment

You have the need to be loved, and when this need is not met, you feel abandoned. Your fear of abandonment drives you to find ways to feel loved.

Life is filled with complex interactions around love. At some point, you will have experiences of feeling abandoned by others, and you will create the experience of abandonment for others. You will perceive abandonment, even when it is not the intention of others, and you will abandon yourself. Your task right now is to identify where this is happening so you can heal that imbalance and align yourself with your true nature.

In its truest and most essential state, love is pure, uncontaminated and unconditional. Challenges arise when we experience love that is not pure and unconditional but enmeshed with rules, duties and obligations. This can manifest as love that is given when it is convenient to the giver, not the receiver. It can also be love that is only shown when you have conformed to the expectations of another or when you think or act the same as this person. None of this is love.

As social beings, we need to experience pure love, give love unconditionally and love ourselves. Love encompasses this trinity within its vibration, and we feel its absence when any part is missing. We interpret this gap as feelings of being unloved, unlovable or abandoned. We search for a solution to these feelings by acting in ways we have learnt will meet our need to be loved.

Journal Prompt

What does love mean to you? Write your own definition of love.
How do you know you are loved? How do others know you love them?
Self-care is an act of self-love. What do you do to take care of yourself?

Empowered Tapping® Script

Use the following script to work through any fears and trauma associated with your past experiences of love and create new possibilities. As you tap each of your meridian points, say this script aloud.

I Accept My Lovability

Round 1 (Repeat twice)

TH: Even though it's normal to want to be loved.

EB: My mind can't just let it be normal.

SE: It has to turn it into an unmet need.

UE: This triggers off my fear response that I will get stuck in my trauma reactions of abandonment.

TL: This then sets off a cascade of emotionally painful and traumatic experiences in my mind's reality.

CH: But it's not how my life really has to be.

CB: It's just my fears running stories from my past.

UB: I don't need certain conditions to exist for me to heal from my experiences of being unloved.

UA: And I don't need specific circumstances to exist for me to transform my fears of abandonment. I already am accepting my lovability.

Round 2

TH: By interpreting my need to be loved, being unmet, sets off post-traumatic stress in me I have created a belief that this is how it is and always will be.

EB: That belief that my need to be loved, being unmet, sets off post-traumatic stress in me is how it is and always will be then colours my experiences, so it feels like it's true.

SE: But it's not true.

UE: By interpreting my need to be loved, being unmet, sets off post-traumatic stress in me I have created a belief that this is how it is and always will be.

TL: That belief that my need to be loved, being unmet, sets off post-traumatic stress in me is how it is and always will be then colours my experiences, so it feels like it's true.

CH: But it's not true.

CB: By interpreting my need to be loved, being unmet, sets off post-traumatic stress in me I have created a belief that this is how it is and always will be.

UB: That belief that my need to be loved, being unmet, sets off post-traumatic stress in me is how it is and always will be then colours my experiences, so it feels like it's true.

UA: But it's not true.

Round 3

TH: By interpreting my fear of abandonment as an expression of post-traumatic stress, I have created a belief that this is how it is and always will be.

EB: That belief that my fear of abandonment, as an expression of post-traumatic stress, is how it is and always will be then colours my experiences, so it feels like it's true.

SE: But it's not true.

UE: By interpreting my fear of abandonment as an expression of post-traumatic stress, I have created a belief that this is how it is and always will be.

TL: That belief that my fear of abandonment, as an expression of post-traumatic stress, is how it is and always will be then colours my experiences, so it feels like it's true.

CH: But it's not true.

CB: By interpreting my fear of abandonment as an expression of post-traumatic stress, I have created a belief that this is how it is and always will be.

UB: That belief that my fear of abandonment, as an expression of post-traumatic stress, is how it is and always will be then colours my experiences, so it feels like it's true.

UA: But it's not true.

Round 4

All points: I'm letting it all go.

Round 5

TH: The only truth is I already am accepting my lovability.

All remaining points: I already am accepting my lovability.

Cycle 2. Belonging/Aloneness

You have the need to belong, and when this need is not met, you feel alone. Your fear that you are alone drives you to find ways to feel like you belong to someone.

Life is filled with complex interactions around belonging. At points in your life, you will experience aloneness due to others' actions, and you will create the experience of aloneness for others. You will perceive aloneness, even when it is not the intention of others, and you will feel alone by yourself. Your task right now is to identify where this is happening so you can heal the imbalance and align yourself with your true nature.

The need to belong is innate and tribal. It is wired into our brains to connect with those around us because thousands of years ago, our survival depended on it. This is our number one need, even more powerful than our need for love. Belonging encompasses the feeling that you are safe, protected, cared for and cared about. A sense of belonging forms when you feel noticed, considered, heard and valued. When you feel different, isolated or that you don't fit in, you identify as an oddity or loner.

Belonging may be entwined with sameness and conformity rather than the acceptance of your unique and individual character. The first step to this healing is making it okay to be you and to belong simultaneously. As you dismantle the rules around belonging and shift your perspectives on being alone, the pain radiating from within will ease. You can then watch who comes into your life and experience the magic of emotional healing.

Journal Prompt

Where in your life do you feel like you don't belong? What are the costs of belonging to those who don't understand you? What about yourself are you uncomfortable with? How can you become comfortable with all of who you are?

Empowered Tapping® Script

Use the following script to work through any fears and trauma associated with your past experiences of belonging to create new possibilities. As you tap each of your meridian points, say this script aloud.

I Belong

Round 1 (Repeat twice)

TH: Even though it's normal to want to belong.

EB: My mind can't just let it be normal.

SE: It has to turn it into an unmet need.

UE: This triggers off my fear responses that I will get stuck in my trauma reactions of aloneness.

TL: This then sets off a cascade of emotionally painful and traumatic experiences in my mind's reality.

CH: But it's not how my life really has to be.

CB: It's just my fears running stories from my past.

UB: I don't need certain conditions to exist for me to heal from my experiences of not belonging.

UA: And I don't need specific circumstances to exist for me to transform my fears of aloneness. I already am forming a sense of belonging to myself and others.

Round 2

TH: By interpreting my need to belong, being unmet, sets off post-traumatic stress in me I have created a belief that this is how it is and always will be.

EB: That belief that my need to belong, being unmet, sets off post-traumatic stress in me is how it is and always will be then colours my experiences, so it feels like it's true.

SE: But it's not true.

UE: By interpreting my need to belong, being unmet, sets off post-traumatic stress in me I have created a belief that this is how it is and always will be.

TL: That belief that my need to belong, being unmet, sets off post-traumatic stress in me is how it is and always will be then colours my experiences, so it feels like it's true.

CH: But it's not true.

CB: By interpreting my need to belong, being unmet, sets off post-traumatic stress in me I have created a belief that this is how it is and always will be.

UB: That belief that my need to belong, being unmet, sets off post-traumatic stress in me is how it is and always will be then colours my experiences, so it feels like it's true.

UA: But it's not true.

Round 3

TH: By interpreting my fear of aloneness as an expression of post-traumatic stress I have created a belief that this is how it is and always will be.

EB: That belief that my fear of aloneness as an expression of post-traumatic stress is how it is and always will be then colours my experiences, so it feels like it's true.

SE: But it's not true.

UE: By interpreting my fear of aloneness as an expression of post-traumatic stress I have created a belief that this is how it is and always will be.

TL: That belief that my fear of aloneness as an expression of post-traumatic stress is how it is and always will be then colours my experiences, so it feels like it's true.

CH: But it's not true.

CB: By interpreting my fear of aloneness as an expression of post-traumatic stress I have created a belief that this is how it is and always will be.

UB: That belief that my fear of aloneness as an expression of post-traumatic stress is how it is and always will be then colours my experiences, so it feels like it's true.

UA: But it's not true.

Round 4

All points: I'm letting it all go.

Round 5

TH: The only truth is I already am forming a sense of belonging to myself and others.

All remaining points: I already am forming a sense of belonging to myself and others.

Cycle 3. Acceptance/Rejection

You have the need to be accepted, and when this need is not met, you feel rejected. Your fear of rejection drives you to find ways to be accepted.

Life is filled with complex interactions around acceptance. At points in your life, you will experience feelings of being rejected by others, and you will create the experience of rejection for others. You will perceive rejection, even when it is not the intention of others, and you will reject yourself. Your task right now is to identify where this is happening so you can heal that imbalance and align yourself with your true nature.

The fear of rejection, which is code for wanting to be accepted, is common to the human experience. It is the undercurrent of people-pleasing and over-adapting to circumstances. Too often, this fear results in a giving up of self as it leads to hiding your true nature, wearing a mask or pretending to be someone you are not. When behaviours, physical attributes, beliefs or personality traits are judged and rejected by others, it feels personal, as if it is about your worth. That's why it hurts so deeply.

Self-acceptance becomes challenging when you internalise your experiences of rejection. Yet, the longer someone else controls your acceptability, the longer you will feel powerless, worthless and judged. Even if you rebel and defiantly try to assert your individuality, that behaviour is coming from an inner sense of rejection. Thus, it creates further unwanted and unproductive responses or experiences. Choice is where power lives. You choose what to do with the details that form your rejection of yourself or others. When you address this fear, accepting and acknowledging your worth can be found in self-awareness, humility and personal growth.

Journal Prompt

What have you done to be accepted that doesn't serve you? Why do others reject you? Why do you reject yourself? What do you plan to do about accepting who you are?

Empowered Tapping® Script

Use the following script to work through any fears and trauma associated with your past experiences of acceptance to create new possibilities. As you tap each of your meridian points, say this script aloud.

I Am Accepted

Round 1 (Repeat twice)

TH: Even though it's normal to want to be accepted.

EB: My mind can't just let it be normal.

SE: It has to turn it into an unmet need.

UE: This triggers off my fear responses that I will get stuck in my trauma reactions of being rejected.

TL: This then sets off a cascade of emotionally painful and traumatic experiences in my mind's reality.

CH: But it's not how my life really has to be.

CB: It's just my fears running stories from my past.

UB: I don't need certain conditions to exist for me to heal from my experiences of being unacceptable.

UA: And I don't need specific circumstances to exist for me to transform my fears of rejection. I already am acceptable.

Round 2

TH: By interpreting my need to be accepted, being unmet, sets off post-traumatic stress in me I have created a belief that this is how it is and always will be.

EB: That belief that my need to be accepted, being unmet, sets off post-traumatic stress in me is how it is and always will be then colours my experiences, so it feels like it's true.

SE: But it's not true.

UE: By interpreting my need to be accepted, being unmet, sets off post-traumatic stress in me I have created a belief that this is how it is and always will be.

TL: That belief that my need to be accepted, being unmet, sets off post-traumatic stress in me is how it is and always will be then colours my experiences, so it feels like it's true.

CH: But it's not true.

CB: By interpreting my need to be accepted, being unmet, sets off post-traumatic stress in me I have created a belief that this is how it is and always will be.

UB: That belief that my need to be accepted, being unmet, sets off post-traumatic stress in me is how it is and always will be then colours my experiences, so it feels like it's true.

UA: But it's not true.

Round 3

TH: By interpreting my fear of rejection as an expression of post-traumatic stress I have created a belief that this is how it is and always will be.

EB: That belief that my fear of rejection as an expression of post-traumatic stress is how it is and always will be then colours my experiences, so it feels like it's true.

SE: But it's not true.

UE: By interpreting my fear of rejection as an expression of post-traumatic stress I have created a belief that this is how it is and always will be.

TL: That belief that my fear of rejection as an expression of post-traumatic stress is how it is and always will be then colours my experiences, so it feels like it's true.

CH: But it's not true.

CB: By interpreting my fear of rejection as an expression of post-traumatic stress I have created a belief that this is how it is and always will be.

UB: That belief that my fear of rejection as an expression of post-traumatic stress is how it is and always will be then colours my experiences, so it feels like it's true.

UA: But it's not true.

Round 4

All points: I'm letting it all go.

Round 5

TH: The only truth is I already am acceptable.

All remaining points: I already am acceptable.

Cycle 4. Approval/Inferiority

You have the need to be approved of, and when this need is not met, you feel that you are not good enough. Your fear of being inferior, less than or not good enough drives you to find ways to be approved of.

Life is filled with complex interactions around approval. There will be times when you experience feelings of not being good enough in the eyes of others, and you will create the experience of inferiority for others. You will perceive that you are being judged as less than, even when that is not the intention of others, and you will feel you are not good enough for yourself. Your task now is to identify where this is happening so you can heal the imbalance and align yourself with your true nature.

The term 'not good enough' is laden with conditions. That is the very first thing to recognise about your need for approval. Gaining approval requires you to meet expectations or requirements — be it someone else's or your own. Approval-seeking is fraught with emotional vulnerability. It's normal to want to be approved of, but the lesson of being good enough is a biggie simply because it is easily entangled in expectation and conditionality.

Humans make mistakes. We don't know things until we learn or experience them, so it's easy to get things wrong before we get them right, and we are imperfect. But to label this as not being good enough, inferior or less than others is cruel and unfair. We are diminished when we do it to others and when we do it to ourselves. Strive to embrace life as a process. When you understand that learning comes in many ways, that you don't need to have all the answers, that it's okay to make mistakes and not to define yourself by the outcomes, you are doing a great job of being human.

Journal Prompt

In what areas do you feel like you are not good enough? Whose voice do you hear in your head saying you are not getting things right? Do you feel you need to be perfect?

Empowered Tapping® Script

Use the following script to work through any fears and trauma associated with your past experiences of approval to create new possibilities. As you tap each of your meridian points, say this script aloud.

I Am Good Enough

Round 1 (Repeat twice)

TH: Even though it's normal to want to be approved of.

EB: My mind can't just let it be normal.

SE: It has to turn it into an unmet need.

UE: This triggers off my fear responses that I will get stuck in my trauma reactions of not being good enough.

TL: This then sets off a cascade of emotionally painful and traumatic experiences in my mind's reality.

CH: But it's not how my life really has to be.

CB: It's just my fears running stories from my past.

UB: I don't need certain conditions to exist for me to heal from my experiences of disapproval.

UA: And I don't need specific circumstances to exist for me to transform my fears of not being good enough. I already am open to being good enough.

Round 2

TH: By interpreting my need to be approved of, being unmet, sets off post-traumatic stress in me I have created a belief that this is how it is and always will be.

EB: That belief that my need to be approved of, being unmet, sets off post-traumatic stress in me is how it is and always will be then colours my experiences, so it feels like it's true.

SE: But it's not true.

UE: By interpreting my need to be approved of, being unmet, sets off post-traumatic stress in me I have created a belief that this is how it is and always will be.

TL: That belief that my need to be approved of, being unmet, sets off post-traumatic stress in me is how it is and always will be then colours my experiences, so it feels like it's true.

CH: But it's not true.

CB: By interpreting my need to be approved of, being unmet, sets off post-traumatic stress in me I have created a belief that this is how it is and always will be.

UB: That belief that my need to be approved of, being unmet, sets off post-traumatic stress in me is how it is and always will be then colours my experiences, so it feels like it's true.

UA: But it's not true.

Round 3

TH: By interpreting my fear of not being good enough as an expression of post-traumatic stress I have created a belief that this is how it is and always will be.

EB: That belief that my fear of not being good enough as an expression of post-traumatic stress is how it is and always will be then colours my experiences, so it feels like it's true.

SE: But it's not true.

UE: By interpreting my fear of not being good enough as an expression of post-traumatic stress I have created a belief that this is how it is and always will be.

TL: That belief that my fear of not being good enough as an expression of post-traumatic stress is how it is and always will be then colours my experiences, so it feels like it's true.

CH: But it's not true.

CB: By interpreting my fear of not being good enough as an expression of post-traumatic stress I have created a belief that this is how it is and always will be.

UB: That belief that my fear of not being good enough as an expression of post-traumatic stress is how it is and always will be then colours my experiences, so it feels like it's true.

UA: But it's not true.

Round 4

All points: I'm letting it all go.

Round 5

TH: The only truth is I already am open to being good enough.

All remaining points: I already am open to being good enough.

Cycle 5. Worthy/Undeserving

You have the need to be worthy, and when this need is not met, you feel undeserving of having what you want. Your fear that you do not deserve the rewards of life drives you to find ways to prove you are worthy.

Life is filled with complex interactions around worthiness. At points in your life, you will have experiences of feeling undeserving of better by others, and you will create the experience of unworthiness for others. You will perceive unworthiness, even when that is not the intention of others, and you will feel undeserving and unworthy to yourself. Your task right now is to identify where this is happening so you can heal the imbalance and align yourself with your true nature.

Your sense of worth is the emotional foundation on which you build the concept of who you are. Without self-worth, everything is built on shaky ground. It's much harder to love and respect yourself, let alone be loved and respected by others. Your self-esteem will fluctuate according to others' judgements of what you do, say and believe. You are worthy because you exist. When you don't know that, you believe you are undeserving of having what you want or dream of.

Procrastination, apathy and fear shackle your imagination, motivation and determination to work towards your potential. Every time you combine your worth with deserving, you keep it conditional and punitive. In your brain, this emotional association with experiences happens all the time. If you believe you deserve the rewards of success, then your brain will equally tell you that you deserve the hardships, the tragedy and the unfair and unjust experiences. If you attach your worth to the rewards or the punishments from the external world, then your worth is conditional. This is a falsehood. You are innately worthy.

Journal Prompt

In what instances do you believe you deserved what happened to you? Do you believe others deserve what happens to them? Do you accept that you are worthy just because you exist? What about others — your children, partners, family, friends, colleagues? Often, we see the good and the lovable in others more than we can see them in ourselves. In what ways are you doing this to keep yourself locked into believing you are unworthy of the life that is yours to live?

Empowered Tapping® Script

Use the following script to work through any fears and trauma associated with your past experiences of worth to create new possibilities. As you tap each of your meridian points, say this script aloud.

I Accept My Worth

Round 1 (Repeat twice)

TH: Even though it's normal to want to be worthy.

EB: My mind can't just let it be normal.

SE: It has to turn it into an unmet need.

UE: This triggers off my fear responses that I will get stuck in my trauma reactions of feeling undeserving of having what I want.

TL: This then sets off a cascade of emotionally painful and traumatic experiences in my mind's reality.

CH: But it's not how my life really has to be.

CB: It's just my fears running stories from my past.

UB: I don't need certain conditions to exist for me to heal from my experiences of unworthiness.

UA: And I don't need specific circumstances to exist for me to transform my fears of undeserving. I already am accepting my worth.

Round 2

TH: By interpreting my need to be worthy, being unmet, sets off post-traumatic stress in me I have created a belief that this is how it is and always will be.

EB: That belief that my need to be worthy, being unmet, sets off post-traumatic stress in me is how it is and always will be then colours my experiences, so it feels like it's true.

SE: But it's not true.

UE: By interpreting my need to be worthy, being unmet, sets off post-traumatic stress in me I have created a belief that this is how it is and always will be.

TL: That belief that my need to be worthy, being unmet, sets off post-traumatic stress in me is how it is and always will be then colours my experiences, so it feels like it's true.

CH: But it's not true.

CB: By interpreting my need to be worthy, being unmet, sets off post-traumatic stress in me I have created a belief that this is how it is and always will be.

UB: That belief that my need to be worthy, being unmet, sets off post-traumatic stress in me is how it is and always will be then colours my experiences, so it feels like it's true.

UA: But it's not true.

Round 3

TH: By interpreting my fear of being undeserving as an expression of post-traumatic stress I have created a belief that this is how it is and always will be.

EB: That belief that my fear of being undeserving as an expression of post-traumatic stress is how it is and always will be then colours my experiences, so it feels like it's true.

SE: But it's not true.

UE: By interpreting my fear of being undeserving as an expression of post-traumatic stress I have created a belief that this is how it is and always will be.

TL: That belief that my fear of being undeserving as an expression of post-traumatic stress is how it is and always will be then colours my experiences, so it feels like it's true.

CH: But it's not true.

CB: By interpreting my fear of being undeserving as an expression of post-traumatic stress I have created a belief that this is how it is and always will be.

UB: That belief that my fear of being undeserving as an expression of post-traumatic stress is how it is and always will be then colours my experiences, so it feels like it's true.

UA: But it's not true.

Round 4

All points: I'm letting it all go.

Round 5

TH: The only truth is I already am accepting my worth.

All remaining points: I already am accepting my worth.

Cycle 6. Okay/Being Wrong

You have the need to feel okay, and when this need is not met, you feel like you can't get anything right. Your fear of being wrong or getting things wrong drives you to find ways to feel okay.

Life is filled with complex interactions around okayness. At points in your life, you will have experiences of feeling wrong instigated by others, and you will create the experience of wrongness for others. You will perceive a judgement of wrongness from others, even when that is not their intention, and you will judge yourself as wrong. Your task right now is to identify where this is happening so you can heal the imbalance and align yourself with your true nature.

Feeling 'okay' is how you describe your worth. Your emotional foundation is the starting place of emotional wellbeing. That foundation is your worth — how okay you feel being you. When you don't feel okay being you, you feel wrong, bad, faulty or flawed. You were born okay. Your worth is innate. A baby doesn't know, or at least shouldn't feel, itself as unworthy or not okay. Then life happens, and your okayness can be smothered. The more you get wrong, the more you get blamed, shamed or in trouble for being a kid, and the more you will internalise that you aren't okay.

The less okay you feel, the less confident you will be, the more you will want acceptance from others, and the more you will try to please others. You will externalise your sense of self and place your personal power into the hands of others. Thus, other's responses to you determine how okay you feel. Your self-esteem rises and falls based on what others say or do to you. How you are treated defines your sense of worth, your degree of okayness. The world is not a happy place when those around you are not validating, loving and nurturing of you. You are okay. It is okay to be human and to grow into your personality, your character traits, your skills, your abilities, your talents and your gifts. Take back your power and decide you are okay for yourself — because you are.

Journal Prompt

Is it okay for you to be you? Where were you shamed and blamed for being you? How do you make others wrong? Is that a reflection of how you feel within?

Empowered Tapping® Script

Use the following script to work through any fears and trauma associated with your past experiences of okayness to create new possibilities. As you tap each of your meridian points, say this script aloud.

I Am Okay

Round 1 (Repeat twice)

TH: Even though it's normal to want to be okay.

EB: My mind can't just let it be normal.

SE: It has to turn it into an unmet need.

UE: This triggers off my fear responses that I will get stuck in my trauma reactions of thinking I can't get anything right.

TL: This then sets off a cascade of emotionally painful and traumatic experiences in my mind's reality.

CH: But it's not how my life really has to be.

CB: It's just my fears running stories from my past.

UB: I don't need certain conditions to exist for me to heal from my experiences of not being okay.

UA: And I don't need specific circumstances to exist for me to transform my fears of not getting anything right. I already am embracing that I'm okay.

Round 2

TH: By interpreting my need to be okay, being unmet, sets off post-traumatic stress in me I have created a belief that this is how it is and always will be.

EB: That belief that my need to be okay, being unmet, sets off post-traumatic stress in me is how it is and always will be then colours my experiences, so it feels like it's true.

SE: But it's not true.

UE: By interpreting my need to be okay, being unmet, sets off post-traumatic stress in me I have created a belief that this is how it is and always will be.

TL: That belief that my need to be okay, being unmet, sets off post-traumatic stress in me is how it is and always will be then colours my experiences, so it feels like it's true.

CH: But it's not true.

CB: By interpreting my need to be okay, being unmet, sets off post-traumatic stress in me I have created a belief that this is how it is and always will be.

UB: That belief that my need to be okay, being unmet, sets off post-traumatic stress in me is how it is and always will be then colours my experiences, so it feels like it's true.

UA: But it's not true.

Round 3

TH: By interpreting my fear that I can't get anything right as an expression of post-traumatic stress I have created a belief that this is how it is and always will be.

EB: That belief that my fear that I can't get anything right as an expression of post-traumatic stress is how it is and always will be then colours my experiences, so it feels like it's true.

SE: But it's not true.

UE: By interpreting my fear that I can't get anything right as an expression of post-traumatic stress I have created a belief that this is how it is and always will be.

TL: That belief that my fear that I can't get anything right as an expression of post-traumatic stress is how it is and always will be then colours my experiences, so it feels like it's true.

CH: But it's not true.

CB: By interpreting my fear that I can't get anything right as an expression of post-traumatic stress I have created a belief that this is how it is and always will be.

UB: That belief that my fear that I can't get anything right as an expression of post-traumatic stress is how it is and always will be then colours my experiences, so it feels like it's true.

UA: But it's not true.

Round 4

All points: I'm letting it all go.

Round 5

TH: The only truth is I already am embracing that I'm okay.

All remaining points: I already am embracing that I'm okay.

Cycle 7. Valued/Invisible

You have the need to be valued, and when this need is not met, you feel invisible. Your fear of invisibility drives you to find ways to be valued.

Life is filled with complex interactions around being valued. At points in your life, you will have experiences of feeling invisible to others, and you will create the experience of invisibility for others. You will perceive invisibility, even when it is not the intention of others, and you will be invisible to yourself. Your task right now is to identify where this is happening so you can heal the imbalance and align yourself with your true nature.

To be valued in the eyes of others, you have to be seen, heard or considered. Someone has to acknowledge you. Wanting your skills, achievements, gifts, talents and abilities to be celebrated and rewarded at the deepest level of your being reflects a need to be valued and respected for absolutely no reason other than because you exist. When this doesn't happen, you feel invisible, like you don't matter, and even worthless. Societal institutions aren't great at valuing people's existence. Over the past thirty years, schools have tried to do this by giving everyone a ribbon or a reward for participating. This hasn't stopped you from feeling invisible. When everyone gets the same reward, there's nothing special about your ribbon, so you still aren't being valued for you.

The acknowledgement of 'you' has to be genuine and proportional. This is where it becomes an inside job. If you can't respect and value yourself, no one can, and even when they try, you will reject it. Own your value, then live in this truth. When you live as your most valuable, special and unique self with no fanfare or ticket parade, you will shine a bright light for all to see. Radiate self-respect and self-belief, and you will be surprised by how quickly you will feel visible and how others are drawn to you.

Journal Prompt

How do you treat yourself? How does your self-talk sound? What do you have to offer the world? What is valuable, special and unique about you?

Empowered Tapping® Script

Use the following script to work through any fears and trauma associated with your past experiences of being valued to create new possibilities. As you tap each of your meridian points, say this script aloud.

I Am Valued

Round 1 (Repeat twice)

TH: Even though it's normal to want to be valued.

EB: My mind can't just let it be normal.

SE: It has to turn it into an unmet need.

UE: This triggers off my fear responses that I will get stuck in my trauma reactions of invisibility.

TL: This then sets off a cascade of emotionally painful and traumatic experiences in my mind's reality.

CH: But it's not how my life really has to be.

CB: It's just my fears running stories from my past.

UB: I don't need certain conditions to exist for me to heal from my experiences of not being valued.

UA: And I don't need specific circumstances to exist for me to transform my fears of invisibility. I already am valued.

Round 2

TH: By interpreting my need to be valued, being unmet, sets off post-traumatic stress in me I have created a belief that this is how it is and always will be.

EB: That belief that my need to be valued, being unmet, sets off post-traumatic stress in me is how it is and always will be then colours my experiences, so it feels like it's true.

SE: But it's not true.

UE: By interpreting my need to be valued, being unmet, sets off post-traumatic stress in me I have created a belief that this is how it is and always will be.

TL: That belief that my need to be valued, being unmet, sets off post-traumatic stress in me is how it is and always will be then colours my experiences, so it feels like it's true.

CH: But it's not true.

CB: By interpreting my need to be valued, being unmet, sets off post-traumatic stress in me I have created a belief that this is how it is and always will be.

UB: That belief that my need to be valued, being unmet, sets off post-traumatic stress in me is how it is and always will be then colours my experiences, so it feels like it's true.

UA: But it's not true.

Round 3

TH: By interpreting my fear of invisibility as an expression of post-traumatic stress I have created a belief that this is how it is and always will be.

EB: That belief that my fear of invisibility as an expression of post-traumatic stress is how it is and always will be then colours my experiences, so it feels like it's true.

SE: But it's not true.

UE: By interpreting my fear of invisibility as an expression of post-traumatic stress I have created a belief that this is how it is and always will be.

TL: That belief that my fear of invisibility as an expression of post-traumatic stress is how it is and always will be then colours my experiences, so it feels like it's true.

CH: But it's not true.

CB: By interpreting my fear of invisibility as an expression of post-traumatic stress I have created a belief that this is how it is and always will be.

UB: That belief that my fear of invisibility as an expression of post-traumatic stress is how it is and always will be then colours my experiences, so it feels like it's true.

UA: But it's not true.

Round 4

All points: I'm letting it all go.

Round 5

TH: The only truth is I already am valued.

All remaining points: I already am valued.

Cycle 8. Equal/Innate Deficit

You have the need to be equal, and when this need is not met, you feel like something is innately wrong with you. This fear drives you to find ways to prove you are of equal worth to others.

Life is filled with complex interactions around equality. At points in your life, you will have experiences of feeling innately bad caused by others, and you will create the experience of inequality for others. You will perceive you are being judged as unequal, even when that is not the intention of others, and you will judge that something is innately wrong within yourself. Your task right now is to identify where this is happening so you can heal the imbalance and align yourself with your true nature.

The very foundation of your self-concept is built on your self-worth. When your worth has been betrayed through abuse, prejudice, abandonment or conditional love, your child-self believes that you must be at fault and that, somehow, there is something innately wrong with you. You don't feel like you are the same as everyone else, and therefore, you are inferior or less than others. What you seek is to be equal. You want to be on an even playing field. You want the same rights, opportunities and freedoms you felt were taken from you, but you see that others have.

As much as society claims we are all equal, you see the inequalities every day. Race, gender, religion, nationality and socioeconomic divisions exist, no matter how subtle they may be. When the media speaks about someone breaking through the glass ceiling, there is an admission of difference, of limitations. This all misses the universal truth that you are of equal worth simply because you exist. Your skills, gifts, talents and even your life's purpose have nothing to do with the fact that you are equal already. No one is better or worse than you. Everyone just is. There is nothing innately wrong with you. Sit with that for a while, then decide what you want that you don't have right now. You are the captain of your ship, and you can achieve success if you put in the effort, have or gain the relevant skills and love the journey you are on.

Journal Prompt

What will change when you accept that you are already equal in worth?

Empowered Tapping® Script

Use the following script to work through any fears and trauma associated with your past experiences of equality to create new possibilities. As you tap each of your meridian points, say this script aloud.

I Am Equal

Round 1 (Repeat twice)

TH: Even though it's normal to want to be equal to others.

EB: My mind can't just let it be normal.

SE: It has to turn it into an unmet need.

UE: This triggers off my fear responses that I will get stuck in my trauma reactions of thinking there is something innately wrong with me.

TL: This then sets off a cascade of emotionally painful and traumatic experiences in my mind's reality.

CH: But it's not how my life really has to be.

CB: It's just my fears running stories from my past.

UB: I don't need certain conditions to exist for me to heal from my experiences of inequality.

UA: And I don't need specific circumstances to exist for me to transform my fears of feeling innately wrong. I already am accepting my equality with all people.

Round 2

TH: By interpreting my need to be equal with others, being unmet, sets off post-traumatic stress in me I have created a belief that this is how it is and always will be.

EB: That belief that my need to be equal with others, being unmet, sets off post-traumatic stress in me is how it is and always will be then colours my experiences, so it feels like it's true.

SE: But it's not true.

UE: By interpreting my need to be equal with others, being unmet, sets off post-traumatic stress in me I have created a belief that this is how it is and always will be.

TL: That belief that my need to be equal with others, being unmet, sets off post-traumatic stress in me is how it is and always will be then colours my experiences, so it feels like it's true.

CH: But it's not true.

CB: By interpreting my need to be equal with others, being unmet, sets off post-traumatic stress in me I have created a belief that this is how it is and always will be.

UB: That belief that my need to be equal with others, being unmet, sets off post-traumatic stress in me is how it is and always will be then colours my experiences, so it feels like it's true.

UA: But it's not true.

Round 3

TH: By interpreting my fear there is something innately wrong with me as an expression of post-traumatic stress I have created a belief that this is how it is and always will be.

EB: That belief that my fear there is something innately wrong with me as an expression of post-traumatic stress is how it is and always will be then colours my experiences, so it feels like it's true.

SE: But it's not true.

UE: By interpreting my fear there is something innately wrong with me as an expression of post-traumatic stress I have created a belief that this is how it is and always will be.

TL: That belief that my fear there is something innately wrong with me as an expression of post-traumatic stress is how it is and always will be then colours my experiences, so it feels like it's true.

CH: But it's not true.

CB: By interpreting my fear there is something innately wrong with me as an expression of post-traumatic stress I have created a belief that this is how it is and always will be.

UB: That belief that my fear there is something innately wrong with me as an expression of post-traumatic stress is how it is and always will be then colours my experiences, so it feels like it's true.

UA: But it's not true.

Round 4

All points: I'm letting it all go.

Round 5

TH: The only truth is I already am accepting my equality with all people.

All remaining points: I already am accepting my equality with all people.

Cycle 9. Needed/Unloved

You have the need to be needed, and when this need is not met, you feel unloved. Your fear that you are unloved drives you to find ways to feel needed.

Life is filled with complex interactions around being needed. At points in your life, you will have experiences of feeling unloved by others, and you will create the experience of being unneeded for others. You will perceive yourself as unneeded, even when that is not the intention of others. And, you will not stand by yourself when you most need yourself to do so. Your task right now is to identify where this is happening so you can heal the imbalance and align yourself with your true nature.

Being needed is something that feeds you. It puts love dollars in your love piggybank. But it is so easy to get trapped by that dopamine hit when you look to be needed constantly or in the same way by the same people. Life changes. People grow up, develop skills and move on. Your role in their lives changes, too. It's not that people don't need you — they do. It might be that they need you in a different way or that new people need you. Being needed by others too often lets you forget about how you are needed by yourself. You need to take care of yourself. True self-love is the capacity to care for you physically, mentally, emotionally, sexually and spiritually. Meeting your needs first enables you to give more freely and unconditionally to others. You can't give from an empty vessel. Nurture yourself. Fill up your tank regularly. Take care of yourself so you can take care of others and enjoy being needed from within and from others.

Journal Prompt

How do you like to give to others? What makes you feel needed? How do you take care of your own needs?

Empowered Tapping® Script

Use the following script to work through any fears and trauma associated with your past experiences of being needed to create new possibilities. As you tap each of your meridian points, say this script aloud.

I Am Needed

Round 1 (Repeat twice)

TH: Even though it's normal to want to be needed.

EB: My mind can't just let it be normal.

SE: It has to turn it into an unmet need.

UE: This triggers off my fear responses that I will get stuck in my trauma reactions of feeling unloved.

TL: This then sets off a cascade of emotionally painful and traumatic experiences in my mind's reality.

CH: But it's not how my life really has to be.

CB: It's just my fears running stories from my past.

UB: I don't need certain conditions to exist for me to heal from my experiences of not being needed.

UA: And I don't need specific circumstances to exist for me to transform my fears of feeling unloved. I already am accepting the ways I am needed.

Round 2

TH: By interpreting my need to be needed, being unmet, sets off post-traumatic stress in me I have created a belief that this is how it is and always will be.

EB: That belief that my need to be needed, being unmet, sets off post-traumatic stress in me is how it is and always will be then colours my experiences, so it feels like it's true.

SE: But it's not true.

UE: By interpreting my need to be needed, being unmet, sets off post-traumatic stress in me I have created a belief that this is how it is and always will be.

TL: That belief that my need to be needed, being unmet, sets off post-traumatic stress in me is how it is and always will be then colours my experiences, so it feels like it's true.

CH: But it's not true.

CB: By interpreting my need to be needed, being unmet, sets off post-traumatic stress in me I have created a belief that this is how it is and always will be.

UB: That belief that my need to be needed, being unmet, sets off post-traumatic stress in me is how it is and always will be then colours my experiences, so it feels like it's true.

UA: But it's not true.

Round 3

TH: By interpreting my fear of feeling unloved as an expression of post-traumatic stress I have created a belief that this is how it is and always will be.

EB: That belief that my fear of feeling unloved as an expression of post-traumatic stress is how it is and always will be then colours my experiences, so it feels like it's true.

SE: But it's not true.

UE: By interpreting my fear of feeling unloved as an expression of post-traumatic stress I have created a belief that this is how it is and always will be.

TL: That belief that my fear of feeling unloved as an expression of post-traumatic stress is how it is and always will be then colours my experiences, so it feels like it's true.

CH: But it's not true.

CB: By interpreting my fear of feeling unloved as an expression of post-traumatic stress I have created a belief that this is how it is and always will be.

UB: That belief that my fear of feeling unloved as an expression of post-traumatic stress is how it is and always will be then colours my experiences, so it feels like it's true.

UA: But it's not true.

Round 4

All points: I'm letting it all go.

Round 5

TH: The only truth is I already am accepting the ways I am needed.

All remaining points: I already am accepting the ways I am needed.

Cycle 10. Safe/Violated

You have the need to be safe, and when this need is not met, you feel violated. Your fear of violation drives you to find ways to ensure your safety.

Life is filled with complex interactions around safety. At points in your life, you will have experiences of feeling violated by others, and you will create the experience of violation for others. You will perceive violation, even when it is not the intention of others, and you will violate yourself. Your task right now is to identify where this is happening so you can heal the imbalance and align yourself with your true nature.

The amygdala has a significant job to do in your brain. It assesses every circumstance, every word and every moment and establishes whether you are safe. It is constantly exploring the environment for cues that you aren't safe physically, emotionally, mentally, socially, sexually and energetically. Even when you are safe, the amygdala will search for anything that could be a risk, including minor things that you are more than capable of managing. When the amygdala finds a threat, it sends messages to your adrenal glands to get ready to fight or run for your life. This can all happen without you having a conscious thought about it. The result of all this activity is that you can feel angry or anxious for reasons recognised and unknown. This is your built-in safety alarm. For it to work effectively, you need to manage it. You don't want to switch it off because when real danger appears, you will be unaware.

Understanding what triggers your amygdala helps you to manage your responses. There could be environmental triggers such as pollution, pollens, electromagnetic disturbances or chemicals. There could be social triggers such as hostile and tense interactions between people, tone of voice, the words spoken and how you are treated or made to feel by others. The triggers may also be internal and fired by what you eat, the types of liquids you drink or your mental chatter. When your inner critic is loud, you may create a sense of being unsafe because you aren't protecting and looking after yourself. If you don't know that you matter or de-value yourself, these beliefs are akin to acts of self-punishment that violate your sense of dignity and worth. Where there is physical danger, you must take action to be safe. Find someone who can act on your behalf if you cannot. This book isn't about physical safety. Here, we are exploring the ways in which your brain perceives danger and how you can work with its responses to support your sense of personal power. Your capacity to act is where your power lies and how you keep yourself safe.

Journal Prompt

In what ways are you creating a sense of being unsafe for yourself? What external triggers create a sense of violation for you?

Empowered Tapping® Script

Use the following script to work through any fears and trauma associated with your past experiences of safety to create new possibilities. As you tap each of your meridian points, say this script aloud.

I Create My Sense of Safety

Round 1 (Repeat twice)

TH: Even though it's normal to want to be safe.

EB: My mind can't just let it be normal.

SE: It has to turn it into an unmet need.

UE: This triggers off my fear responses that I will get stuck in my trauma reactions of feeling violated.

TL: This then sets off a cascade of emotionally painful and traumatic experiences in my mind's reality.

CH: But it's not how my life really has to be.

CB: It's just my fears running stories from my past.

UB: I don't need certain conditions to exist for me to heal from my experiences of feeling unsafe.

UA: And I don't need specific circumstances to exist for me to transform my fears of violation. I already am creating my internal sense of safety.

Round 2

TH: By interpreting my need to be safe, being unmet, sets off post-traumatic stress in me I have created a belief that this is how it is and always will be.

EB: That belief that my need to be safe, being unmet, sets off post-traumatic stress in me is how it is and always will be then colours my experiences, so it feels like it's true.

SE: But it's not true.

UE: By interpreting my need to be safe, being unmet, sets off post-traumatic stress in me I have created a belief that this is how it is and always will be.

TL: That belief that my need to be safe, being unmet, sets off post-traumatic stress in me is how it is and always will be then colours my experiences, so it feels like it's true.

CH: But it's not true.

CB: By interpreting my need to be safe, being unmet, sets off post-traumatic stress in me I have created a belief that this is how it is and always will be.

UB: That belief that my need to be safe, being unmet, sets off post-traumatic stress in me is how it is and always will be then colours my experiences, so it feels like it's true.

UA: But it's not true.

Round 3

TH: By interpreting my fear of violation as an expression of post-traumatic stress I have created a belief that this is how it is and always will be.

EB: That belief that my fear of violation as an expression of post-traumatic stress is how it is and always will be then colours my experiences, so it feels like it's true.

SE: But it's not true.

UE: By interpreting my fear of violation as an expression of post-traumatic stress I have created a belief that this is how it is and always will be.

TL: That belief that my fear of violation as an expression of post-traumatic stress is how it is and always will be then colours my experiences, so it feels like it's true.

CH: But it's not true.

CB: By interpreting my fear of violation as an expression of post-traumatic stress I have created a belief that this is how it is and always will be.

UB: That belief that my fear of violation as an expression of post-traumatic stress is how it is and always will be then colours my experiences, so it feels like it's true.

UA: But it's not true.

Round 4

All points: I'm letting it all go.

Round 5

TH: The only truth is I already am creating my internal sense of safety.

All remaining points: I already am creating my internal sense of safety.

Cycle 11. Existing/Unwanted

You have the need to exist, and when this need is not met, you feel unwanted. Your fear of being unwanted drives you to find ways to feel like you exist.

Life is filled with complex interactions around your existence. At points in your life, you will have experiences of feeling unwanted by others, and you will create the experience of being unwanted for others. You will feel unwanted, even when that is not the intention of others, and you will ignore your own existence. Your task right now is to identify where this is happening so you can heal the imbalance and align yourself with your true nature.

Too often, people dismiss the need to exist because they focus on flesh and blood. You physically exist, so you can't feel like you don't exist. But when you arrived in the physical world at birth, you were new to having a body separate from your mother. You had to form an idea of existing. You looked for validation — for evidence that you really did exist and took up space in your own right. You emotionally processed this with the feeling of being wanted. Whenever you don't feel like your needs are being met, it can trigger feelings of being unwanted, as if you don't exist or are invisible. This impacts your capacity to be present in the immediate moment and to take up space. You might be quiet, socially awkward or shy as a result. You might dull your shine or limit your successes because you haven't owned your right to exist as a unique presence in the world. Instead, you play small and act out a lesser version of yourself. Sometimes, you may not even want to be you. The pain is real, and the answer lives inside of you. You want to be the very best version of yourself. Humanistic psychologists have theorised for decades that we all have an internal drive to be more. That is, we innately want to give purpose to our existence and to live it fully. You are here. You do exist for a reason.

Journal Prompt

When do you play small? What makes you want to shrink? What would a better version of you look like right now?

Empowered Tapping® Script

Use the following script to work through any fears and trauma associated with your past experiences of existence to create new possibilities. As you tap each of your meridian points, say this script aloud.

I Exist

Round 1 (Repeat twice)

TH: Even though it's normal to want to exist.

EB: My mind can't just let it be normal.

SE: It has to turn it into an unmet need.

UE: This triggers off my fear responses that I will get stuck in my trauma reactions of feeling unwanted.

TL: This then sets off a cascade of emotionally painful and traumatic experiences in my mind's reality.

CH: But it's not how my life really has to be.

CB: It's just my fears running stories from my past.

UB: I don't need certain conditions to exist for me to heal from my experiences of non-existence.

UA: And I don't need specific circumstances to exist for me to transform my fears of being unwanted. I already am accepting my experiences of existing.

Round 2

TH: By interpreting my need to exist, being unmet, sets off post-traumatic stress in me I have created a belief that this is how it is and always will be.

EB: That belief that my need to exist, being unmet, sets off post-traumatic stress in me is how it is and always will be then colours my experiences, so it feels like it's true.

SE: But it's not true.

UE: By interpreting my need to exist, being unmet, sets off post-traumatic stress in me I have created a belief that this is how it is and always will be.

TL: That belief that my need to exist, being unmet, sets off post-traumatic stress in me is how it is and always will be then colours my experiences, so it feels like it's true.

CH: But it's not true.

CB: By interpreting my need to exist, being unmet, sets off post-traumatic stress in me I have created a belief that this is how it is and always will be.

UB: That belief that my need to exist, being unmet, sets off post-traumatic stress in me is how it is and always will be then colours my experiences, so it feels like it's true.

UA: But it's not true.

Round 3

TH: By interpreting my fear of being unwanted as an expression of post-traumatic stress I have created a belief that this is how it is and always will be.

EB: That belief that my fear of being unwanted as an expression of post-traumatic stress is how it is and always will be then colours my experiences, so it feels like it's true.

SE: But it's not true.

UE: By interpreting my fear of being unwanted as an expression of post-traumatic stress I have created a belief that this is how it is and always will be.

TL: That belief that my fear of being unwanted as an expression of post-traumatic stress is how it is and always will be then colours my experiences, so it feels like it's true.

CH: But it's not true.

CB: By interpreting my fear of being unwanted as an expression of post-traumatic stress I have created a belief that this is how it is and always will be.

UB: That belief that my fear of being unwanted as an expression of post-traumatic stress is how it is and always will be then colours my experiences, so it feels like it's true.

UA: But it's not true.

Round 4

All points: I'm letting it all go.

Round 5

TH: The only truth is I already am accepting my experiences of existing.

All remaining points: I already am accepting my experiences of my existing.

Cycle 12. Competent/Inadequate

You have the need to feel competent, and when this need is not met, you feel inadequate. Your fear of inadequacy and failure drives you to find ways to feel competent.

Life is filled with complex interactions around competency. At points in your life, you will have experiences of feeling inadequate, and you will create the experience of inadequacy for others. You will perceive inadequacy, even when it is not the intention of others, and you will feel like you have failed yourself. Your task right now is to identify where this is happening so you can heal the imbalance and align yourself with your true nature.

The desire to feel competent is a multi-layered experience. You could be skilled in one area of your life, yet not another. Then there is the reality that everything has greater depths, so while you may be competent at a particular level, there is constant room for improvement. New ways and knowledge are being discovered all the time. Growth is life. It's so easy to end up feeling inadequate. But feeling like a failure doesn't serve or help you be all you can be. Embrace the evolving nature of life, of being you. Strive to learn and grow by practising new skills and talents and discover gifts you didn't even know you had. Take on the adventure of not knowing. Get comfortable with the vulnerability it creates and discover how it fuels your imagination and inspires you to dive deeper into life. You can learn anything, and if it turns out that there are things you're just not great at, that's okay, too. That doesn't make you a failure or inadequate. It makes you human.

Journal Prompt

What do you want to be more competent at or in? What skills do you need to develop? Make a plan to learn the skills you need and put in the effort to improve.

Empowered Tapping® Script

Use the following script to work through any fears and trauma associated with your past experiences of competency to create new possibilities. As you tap each of your meridian points, say this script aloud.

I Am Competent

Round 1 (Repeat twice)

TH: Even though it's normal to want to feel competent in my skills.

EB: My mind can't just let it be normal.

SE: It has to turn it into an unmet need.

UE: This triggers off my fear responses that I will get stuck in my trauma reactions of inadequacy.

TL: This then sets off a cascade of emotionally painful and traumatic experiences in my mind's reality.

CH: But it's not how my life really has to be.

CB: It's just my fears running stories from my past.

UB: I don't need certain conditions to exist for me to heal from my experiences of inadequacy.

UA: And I don't need specific circumstances to exist for me to transform my fears of inadequacy. I already am accepting my competencies.

Round 2

TH: By interpreting my need to feel competent in my skills, being unmet, sets off post-traumatic stress in me I have created a belief that this is how it is and always will be.

EB: That belief that my need to feel competent in my skills, being unmet, sets off post-traumatic stress in me is how it is and always will be then colours my experiences, so it feels like it's true.

SE: But it's not true.

UE: By interpreting my need to feel competent in my skills, being unmet, sets off post-traumatic stress in me I have created a belief that this is how it is and always will be.

TL: That belief that my need to feel competent in my skills, being unmet, sets off post-traumatic stress in me is how it is and always will be then colours my experiences, so it feels like it's true.

CH: But it's not true.

CB: By interpreting my need to feel competent in my skills, being unmet, sets off post-traumatic stress in me I have created a belief that this is how it is and always will be.

UB: That belief that my need to feel competent in my skills, being unmet, sets off post-traumatic stress in me is how it is and always will be then colours my experiences, so it feels like it's true.

UA: But it's not true.

Round 3

TH: By interpreting my fear of inadequacy as an expression of post-traumatic stress I have created a belief that this is how it is and always will be.

EB: That belief that my fear of inadequacy as an expression of post-traumatic stress is how it is and always will be then colours my experiences, so it feels like it's true.

SE: But it's not true.

UE: By interpreting my fear of inadequacy as an expression of post-traumatic stress I have created a belief that this is how it is and always will be.

TL: That belief that my fear of inadequacy as an expression of post-traumatic stress is how it is and always will be then colours my experiences, so it feels like it's true.

CH: But it's not true.

CB: By interpreting my fear of inadequacy as an expression of post-traumatic stress I have created a belief that this is how it is and always will be.

UB: That belief that my fear of inadequacy as an expression of post-traumatic stress is how it is and always will be then colours my experiences, so it feels like it's true.

UA: But it's not true.

Round 4

All points: I'm letting it all go.

Round 5

TH: The only truth is I already am accepting my competencies.

All remaining points: I already am accepting my competencies.

Cycle 13. Dignity/Faulty

You have the need to have a sense of dignity, and when this need is not met, you feel faulty. Your fear of being faulty drives you to find ways to have a sense of dignity.

Life is filled with complex interactions around dignity. At points in your life, you will have experiences of feeling faulty as judged by others, and you will create the experience of faultiness for others. You will perceive faultiness, even when it is not the intention of others, and you will judge yourself as faulty. Your task right now is to identify where this is happening so you can heal the imbalance and align yourself with your true nature.

Your sense of dignity encases your sense of worth, equality and value in the package that is you. There is an idea that your dignity is an inalienable truth that cannot be denied. To have dignity is to have sovereignty over yourself. It means that you are free and cannot be a slave to another or society. So, each time you subjugate yourself, conform when you don't want to, betray your truth or try to keep someone happy, you are left with a hint of blame from within and from the external world that leaves you feeling faulty.

You may feel like something is innately wrong with you and live with a consistent sense of being flawed, faulty or weak. When your inner critic piles on the self-blame, you may feel broken and fragile. Over time, you can lose connection with your sense of dignity and with having a limit to what you will tolerate and how much you will put up with. You forget your own humanity and the outer world feels inhumane. This violation of self cuts to the core of who you are. No matter how far removed you feel, your sense of dignity is always there. The value of your existence is immeasurable. Your autonomy, your self-determination and your capacity to be complete in your dominion are just waiting for you to be brave enough to own them.

Journal Prompt

Where have you conformed when you didn't want to? What are the signs that you are violating your dignity?

Empowered Tapping® Script

Use the following script to work through any fears and trauma associated with your past experiences of dignity to create new possibilities. As you tap each of your meridian points, say this script aloud.

I Have Dignity

Round 1 (Repeat twice)

TH: Even though it's normal to want to create an internal sense of dignity.

EB: My mind can't just let it be normal.

SE: It has to turn it into an unmet need.

UE: This triggers off my fear responses that I will get stuck in my trauma reactions of feeling faulty.

TL: This then sets off a cascade of emotionally painful and traumatic experiences in my mind's reality.

CH: But it's not how my life really has to be.

CB: It's just my fears running stories from my past.

UB: I don't need certain conditions to exist for me to heal from the experiences that violated my dignity.

UA: And I don't need specific circumstances to exist for me to transform my fears of being faulty. I already am creating my internal sense of dignity.

Round 2

TH: By interpreting my need to create an internal sense of dignity, being unmet, sets off post-traumatic stress in me I have created a belief that this is how it is and always will be.

EB: That belief that my need to create an internal sense of dignity, being unmet, sets off post-traumatic stress in me is how it is and always will be then colours my experiences, so it feels like it's true.

SE: But it's not true.

UE: By interpreting my need to create an internal sense of dignity, being unmet, sets off post-traumatic stress in me I have created a belief that this is how it is and always will be.

TL: That belief that my need to create an internal sense of dignity, being unmet, sets off post-traumatic stress in me is how it is and always will be then colours my experiences, so it feels like it's true.

CH: But it's not true.

CB: By interpreting my need to create an internal sense of dignity, being unmet, sets off post-traumatic stress in me I have created a belief that this is how it is and always will be.

UB: That belief that my need to create an internal sense of dignity, being unmet, sets off post-traumatic stress in me is how it is and always will be then colours my experiences, so it feels like it's true.

UA: But it's not true.

Round 3

TH: By interpreting my fear of being faulty as an expression of post-traumatic stress I have created a belief that this is how it is and always will be.

EB: That belief that my fear of being faulty as an expression of post-traumatic stress is how it is and always will be then colours my experiences, so it feels like it's true.

SE: But it's not true.

UE: By interpreting my fear of being faulty as an expression of post-traumatic stress I have created a belief that this is how it is and always will be.

TL: That belief that my fear of being faulty as an expression of post-traumatic stress is how it is and always will be then colours my experiences, so it feels like it's true.

CH: But it's not true.

CB: By interpreting my fear of being faulty as an expression of post-traumatic stress I have created a belief that this is how it is and always will be.

UB: That belief that my fear of being faulty as an expression of post-traumatic stress is how it is and always will be then colours my experiences, so it feels like it's true.

UA: But it's not true.

Round 4

All points: I'm letting it all go.

Round 5

TH: The only truth is I already am creating my internal sense of dignity.

All remaining points: I already am creating my internal sense of dignity.

Cycle 14. Protected/Powerless

You have the need to be protected, and when this need is not met, you feel powerless. Your fear of powerlessness drives you to find ways to be protected.

Life is filled with complex interactions around protection. At points in your life, you will have experiences of feeling unprotected by others, and you will create the experience of not protecting others. You will perceive being unprotected, even when it is not the intention of others, and you will not protect yourself when it is your responsibility to do so. Your task right now is to identify where this is happening so you can heal the imbalance and align yourself with your true nature.

It's easy to merge a sense of safety with being protected because they overlap. But there is an experience around protection that is specific and important for you to recognise. Power is defined as the ability to act. Therefore, feeling powerless means you don't feel like you *can* act. If you can't act, you can't protect yourself or others. The statistics on domestic violence and child sexual assault indicate how common these incidences occur, so the issue of protection and powerlessness has monumental importance for yourself and society. The ability to speak up, take action, say no and walk away from unhealthy, disrespectful and dangerous interactions is paramount. But where do we learn how to do this? Ideally, families would role model it and, at the right times, teach the skills, nurture your intuitive hunches and support your sense of inner authority.

What happens when parents haven't learnt those skills? They can't teach what they don't know. Schools usually end up with the responsibility, but it's not ideal. Self-defence or martial arts classes can be invaluable. As much as we may think being protective and acting protectively is innate, it isn't. It's easy to feel powerless in a threatening scenario. Any number of circumstances can result in you not protecting another or not acting to protect yourself but instead feeling powerless. The solution starts with your sense of self-worth and knowing you have the right to protect yourself. When both these aspects of self are in tatters, begin repairing them and move on from there.

Journal Prompt

Who didn't act to protect you? What have you learnt from this experience?

Empowered Tapping® Script

Use the following script to work through any fears and trauma associated with your past experiences of protection to create new possibilities. As you tap each of your meridian points, say this script aloud.

I Am Protected

Round 1 (Repeat twice)

TH: Even though it's normal to want to be protected.

EB: My mind can't just let it be normal.

SE: It has to turn it into an unmet need.

UE: This triggers off my fear responses that I will get stuck in my trauma reactions of feeling powerless.

TL: This then sets off a cascade of emotionally painful and traumatic experiences in my mind's reality.

CH: But it's not how my life really has to be.

CB: It's just my fears running stories from my past.

UB: I don't need certain conditions to exist for me to heal from my experiences of being unprotected.

UA: And I don't need specific circumstances to exist for me to transform my fears of powerlessness. I already am allowing myself to be protected.

Round 2

TH: By interpreting my need to be protected, being unmet, sets off post-traumatic stress in me I have created a belief that this is how it is and always will be.

EB: That belief that my need to be protected, being unmet, sets off post-traumatic stress in me is how it is and always will be then colours my experiences, so it feels like it's true.

SE: But it's not true.

UE: By interpreting my need to be protected, being unmet, sets off post-traumatic stress in me I have created a belief that this is how it is and always will be.

TL: That belief that my need to be protected, being unmet, sets off post-traumatic stress in me is how it is and always will be then colours my experiences, so it feels like it's true.

CH: But it's not true.

CB: By interpreting my need to be protected, being unmet, sets off post-traumatic stress in me I have created a belief that this is how it is and always will be.

UB: That belief that my need to be protected, being unmet, sets off post-traumatic stress in me is how it is and always will be then colours my experiences, so it feels like it's true.

UA: But it's not true.

Round 3

TH: By interpreting my fear of powerlessness as an expression of post-traumatic stress I have created a belief that this is how it is and always will be.

EB: That belief that my fear of powerlessness as an expression of post-traumatic stress is how it is and always will be then colours my experiences, so it feels like it's true.

SE: But it's not true.

UE: By interpreting my fear of powerlessness as an expression of post-traumatic stress I have created a belief that this is how it is and always will be.

TL: That belief that my fear of powerlessness as an expression of post-traumatic stress is how it is and always will be then colours my experiences, so it feels like it's true.

CH: But it's not true.

CB: By interpreting my fear of powerlessness as an expression of post-traumatic stress I have created a belief that this is how it is and always will be.

UB: That belief that my fear of powerlessness as an expression of post-traumatic stress is how it is and always will be then colours my experiences, so it feels like it's true.

UA: But it's not true.

Round 4

All points: I'm letting it all go.

Round 5

TH: The only truth is I already am allowing myself to be protected.

All remaining points: I already am allowing myself to be protected.

Cycle 15. Security/Lack

You have the need to feel secure, and when this need is not met, you suffer insecurity. Your fear of lack drives you to find ways to create a sense of security.

Life is filled with complex interactions around security. At points in your life, you will have experiences of feeling insecure with others, and you will create the experience of insecurity for others. You will perceive lack, even when it is not the intention of others, and you will feel insecure within yourself. Your task right now is to identify where this is happening so you can heal the imbalance and align yourself with your true nature.

The number one fear is lack. We perceive lack within the first two years of life, and our fear of missing out begins. It's not the result of how you were raised but an internal, in-built mechanism for humans. We all have it. Advertisers know this and work it to get you to buy their products. It is very easy to have FOMO—fear of missing out—or a keeping-up-with-the-Jones' mentality. When we were living in caves and facing sabre-toothed tigers, this sense of lack worked in our favour as it motivated us to survive, to look for more in the form of safer places to sleep at night, better sources of food and clean and plentiful water sources.

In today's world, this in-built survival mechanism can become a self-sabotaging insecurity that feeds your suffering. But it doesn't have to. You can manage this inner drive. In a modern society, there are opportunities to grow beyond the needs of survival — and to flourish. Abraham Maslow spoke about our higher needs of love, belonging, esteem and self-actualisation. You can be realistic about what you need to be happy and live within your means. You can be grateful for all you have and bloom. You can set budgets, work towards your goals and manifest your dreams with joy and appreciation for all you have. When you do this, insecurity evaporates.

Journal Prompt

Do you suffer from FOMO (Fear of Missing Out)? Are you busy ensuring you have everything the same as someone you admire? Is that helping you live your best life?

Empowered Tapping® Script

Use the following script to work through any fears and trauma associated with your past experiences of security to create new possibilities. As you tap each of your meridian points, say this script aloud.

I Am Secure

Round 1 (Repeat twice)

TH: Even though it's normal to want to feel secure.

EB: My mind can't just let it be normal.

SE: It has to turn it into an unmet need.

UE: This triggers off my fear responses that I will get stuck in my trauma reactions of insecurity.

TL: This then sets off a cascade of emotionally painful and traumatic experiences in my mind's reality.

CH: But it's not how my life really has to be.

CB: It's just my fears running stories from my past.

UB: I don't need certain conditions to exist for me to heal from my experiences of not feeling secure.

UA: And I don't need specific circumstances to exist for me to transform my fears of insecurity. I already am feeling secure within.

Round 2

TH: By interpreting my need to feel secure, being unmet, sets off post-traumatic stress in me I have created a belief that this is how it is and always will be.

EB: That belief that my need to feel secure, being unmet, sets off post-traumatic stress in me is how it is and always will be then colours my experiences, so it feels like it's true.

SE: But it's not true.

UE: By interpreting my need to feel secure, being unmet, sets off post-traumatic stress in me I have created a belief that this is how it is and always will be.

TL: That belief that my need to feel secure, being unmet, sets off post-traumatic stress in me is how it is and always will be then colours my experiences, so it feels like it's true.

CH: But it's not true.

CB: By interpreting my need to feel secure, being unmet, sets off post-traumatic stress in me I have created a belief that this is how it is and always will be.

UB: That belief that my need to feel secure, being unmet, sets off post-traumatic stress in me is how it is and always will be then colours my experiences, so it feels like it's true.

UA: But it's not true.

Round 3

TH: By interpreting my fear of insecurity as an expression of post-traumatic stress I have created a belief that this is how it is and always will be.

EB: That belief that my fear of insecurity as an expression of post-traumatic stress is how it is and always will be then colours my experiences, so it feels like it's true.

SE: But it's not true.

UE: By interpreting my fear of insecurity as an expression of post-traumatic stress I have created a belief that this is how it is and always will be.

TL: That belief that my fear of insecurity as an expression of post-traumatic stress is how it is and always will be then colours my experiences, so it feels like it's true.

CH: But it's not true.

CB: By interpreting my fear of insecurity as an expression of post-traumatic stress I have created a belief that this is how it is and always will be.

UB: That belief that my fear of insecurity as an expression of post-traumatic stress is how it is and always will be then colours my experiences, so it feels like it's true.

UA: But it's not true.

Round 4

All points: I'm letting it all go.

Round 5

TH: The only truth is I already am feeling secure within.

All remaining points: I already am feeling secure within.

Cycle 16. Significance/Insignificance

You have the need to matter, and when this need is not met, you feel insignificant. Your fear of insignificance drives you to find ways to feel like you matter.

Life is filled with complex interactions around feeling significant. At points in your life, you will have experiences of feeling insignificant to others, and you will create the experience of insignificance for others. You will perceive insignificance, even when it is not the intention of others, and you will not matter to yourself. Your task right now is to identify where this is happening so you can heal the imbalance and align yourself with your true nature.

We all require our basic emotional needs to be met in two ways — from ourselves and by others. You are no different. The interactions and types of relationships you have with people matter to you. The tone of voice you speak with, your presence when listening and the time you spend with others show people that they matter to you. Your actions, words and behaviours demonstrate that they are a significant and valued part of your life. Because you care for and about them, you are open to sharing who you are, including your innermost joys and fears. This forms part of our sense of belonging. To feel like you matter to others, you look for the same behaviours being demonstrated to you. When this doesn't happen, you fear that you are insignificant and don't matter to them. This can create a sense that the relationship is not equal and make you feel vulnerable to being hurt or betrayed.

How people learn to treat us is influenced by how we treat ourselves. When you don't matter to you, there will be those who don't treat you with respect. Your self-talk is the key to identifying how much you value yourself. What does your mind tell you about you? The more negative your self-talk is, the more insignificant you will feel. A harsh inner critic that dismisses everything you do or say, nit-picks every flaw or mistake and belittles your worth in the world, makes life hard. Those with a critical inner voice are less likely to take care of themselves, set healthy boundaries or have the confidence to be all they can be. When you don't prioritise yourself, you are telling yourself and the world around you that you don't matter, that you are insignificant. It simply isn't true. You do matter. You are significant. It's time for you to believe this, so you act from that truth.

Journal Prompt

What specifically does your inner critic say to you? Identify who that voice reminds you of. If it is you, what can you do to be kinder to yourself? If it is another person, will you continue to let them dominate and control your happiness? What can you do to change?

Empowered Tapping® Script

Use the following script to work through any fears and trauma associated with your past experiences of significance to create new possibilities. As you tap each of your meridian points, say this script aloud.

I Matter

Round 1 (Repeat twice)

TH: Even though it's normal to want to matter.

EB: My mind can't just let it be normal.

SE: It has to turn it into an unmet need.

UE: This triggers off my fear responses that I will get stuck in my trauma reactions of feeling insignificant.

TL: This then sets off a cascade of emotionally painful and traumatic experiences in my mind's reality.

CH: But it's not how my life really has to be.

CB: It's just my fears running stories from my past.

UB: I don't need certain conditions to exist for me to heal from my experiences of not mattering.

UA: And I don't need specific circumstances to exist for me to transform my fears of insignificance. I already am accepting that I matter.

Round 2

TH: By interpreting my need to matter, being unmet, sets off post-traumatic stress in me I have created a belief that this is how it is and always will be.

EB: That belief that my need to matter, being unmet, sets off post-traumatic stress in me is how it is and always will be then colours my experiences, so it feels like it's true.

SE: But it's not true.

UE: By interpreting my need to matter, being unmet, sets off post-traumatic stress in me I have created a belief that this is how it is and always will be.

TL: That belief that my need to matter, being unmet, sets off post-traumatic stress in me is how it is and always will be then colours my experiences, so it feels like it's true.

CH: But it's not true.

CB: By interpreting my need to matter, being unmet, sets off post-traumatic stress in me I have created a belief that this is how it is and always will be.

UB: That belief that my need to matter, being unmet, sets off post-traumatic stress in me is how it is and always will be then colours my experiences, so it feels like it's true.

UA: But it's not true.

Round 3

TH: By interpreting my fear of insignificance as an expression of post-traumatic stress I have created a belief that this is how it is and always will be.

EB: That belief that my fear of insignificance as an expression of post-traumatic stress is how it is and always will be then colours my experiences, so it feels like it's true.

SE: But it's not true.

UE: By interpreting my fear of insignificance as an expression of post-traumatic stress I have created a belief that this is how it is and always will be.

TL: That belief that my fear of insignificance as an expression of post-traumatic stress is how it is and always will be then colours my experiences, so it feels like it's true.

CH: But it's not true.

CB: By interpreting my fear of insignificance as an expression of post-traumatic stress I have created a belief that this is how it is and always will be.

UB: That belief that my fear of insignificance as an expression of post-traumatic stress is how it is and always will be then colours my experiences, so it feels like it's true.

UA: But it's not true.

Round 4

All points: I'm letting it all go.

Round 5

TH: The only truth is I already am accepting that I matter.

All remaining points: I already am accepting that I matter.

Cycle 17. Honesty/Deception

You have the need for honesty, and when this need is not met, you feel deceived. Your fear of being deceived drives you to find ways to discover the truth.

Life is filled with complex interactions around honesty. At points in your life, you will have experiences of feeling deceived by others, and you will create the experience of deception for others. You will perceive deception, even when it is not the intention of others, and you will deceive yourself. Your task right now is to identify where this is happening so you can heal the imbalance and align yourself with your true nature.

Honesty is a profoundly complex quality because you are a social being. You can't always be honest about everything because you will hurt other's feelings. Likewise, as much as you want others to be honest with you, your feelings could get hurt. In *Making Sense of the Insensible,* I say, "The injustice of deception lies in its denial, not in its existence." Whether at a societal or personal level, decide where you want honesty. You can ask for transparency in all matters, but be ready to be mature and responsible enough to manage what it reveals. What matters to you? Where do you want honesty to be a priority?

Conversely, you also decide how much deception you want to live with. Privacy issues can become tangled in honesty and leave you vulnerable to manipulation or harm. You have a right to protect yourself. This is where your values influence your experiences and can create disharmony in your emotional nature. Imagine you want honesty to be a priority in your intimate relationships, but equally, you want trust and respect. Your partner has been told a confidential, private piece of information from a lifelong friend. Do you want them to tell you, even if it requires them to break that friend's trust?

Honesty and deception are complex, multi-layered experiences in the outside world. But what about honesty with yourself? This isn't complex. The more honest you are with yourself, providing it is realistic and not a barrage from your self-critic or coping mechanisms, the better you will manage human interactions. You will always be learning about yourself, discovering who you are and what is possible for you. When you relate to yourself with self-respect, self-love and self-compassion, you will be more honest and less self-deceptive. Sigmond Freud spoke of defence mechanisms such as compensation, repression, denial, fantasy, isolation, projection, reaction formation and rationalisation that humans use to disconnect themselves from the uncomfortable aspects of their personalities. Honesty asks you to embrace your shadow, love all of you, and, when your coping mechanisms don't serve you, to heal them.

Journal Prompt

What are your rules about honesty? Where are you willing to be deceived? How are you honest with yourself?

Empowered Tapping® Script

Use the following script to work through any fears and trauma associated with your past experiences of honesty to create new possibilities. As you tap each of your meridian points, say this script aloud.

I Emanate Honesty

Round 1 (Repeat twice)

TH: Even though it's normal to want honesty in my interactions.

EB: My mind can't just let it be normal.

SE: It has to turn it into an unmet need.

UE: This triggers off my fear responses that I will get stuck in my trauma reactions of feeling deceived.

TL: This then sets off a cascade of emotionally painful and traumatic experiences in my mind's reality.

CH: But it's not how my life really has to be.

CB: It's just my fears running stories from my past.

UB: I don't need certain conditions to exist for me to heal from my experiences of dishonesty.

UA: And I don't need specific circumstances to exist for me to transform my fears of deception. I already am emanating honesty.

Round 2

TH: By interpreting my need for honesty, being unmet, sets off post-traumatic stress in me I have created a belief that this is how it is and always will be.

EB: That belief that my need for honesty, being unmet, sets off post-traumatic stress in me is how it is and always will be then colours my experiences, so it feels like it's true.

SE: But it's not true.

UE: By interpreting my need for honesty, being unmet, sets off post-traumatic stress in me I have created a belief that this is how it is and always will be.

TL: That belief that my need for honesty, being unmet, sets off post-traumatic stress in me is how it is and always will be then colours my experiences, so it feels like it's true.

CH: But it's not true.

CB: By interpreting my need for honesty, being unmet, sets off post-traumatic stress in me I have created a belief that this is how it is and always will be.

UB: That belief that my need for honesty, being unmet, sets off post-traumatic stress in me is how it is and always will be then colours my experiences, so it feels like it's true.

UA: But it's not true.

Round 3

TH: By interpreting my fear of being deceived as an expression of post-traumatic stress I have created a belief that this is how it is and always will be.

EB: That belief that my fear of being deceived as an expression of post-traumatic stress is how it is and always will be then colours my experiences, so it feels like it's true.

SE: But it's not true.

UE: By interpreting my fear of being deceived as an expression of post-traumatic stress I have created a belief that this is how it is and always will be.

TL: That belief that my fear of being deceived as an expression of post-traumatic stress is how it is and always will be then colours my experiences, so it feels like it's true.

CH: But it's not true.

CB: By interpreting my fear of being deceived as an expression of post-traumatic stress I have created a belief that this is how it is and always will be.

UB: That belief that my fear of being deceived as an expression of post-traumatic stress is how it is and always will be then colours my experiences, so it feels like it's true.

UA: But it's not true.

Round 4

All points: I'm letting it all go.

Round 5

TH: The only truth is I already am emanating honesty.

All remaining points: I already am emanating honesty.

Cycle 18. Respected/Overlooked

You have the need to be respected, and when this need is not met, you feel overlooked. Your fear of being overlooked drives you to find ways to be respected.

Life is filled with complex interactions around respect. At points in your life, you will have experiences of feeling disrespected by others, and you will create the experience of disrespect for others. You will perceive disrespect, even when it is not the intention of others, and you will disrespect yourself. Your task right now is to identify where this is happening so you can heal the imbalance and align yourself with your true nature.

Respect is being prized simply because you exist. Respect is conveyed through tone of voice, the warmth of a look or an understanding touch of a hand. In other words, you can feel disrespected because of how you were spoken to, looked at or touched. Previous generations were taught that respect was automatic. Children were raised to respect their parents, elders and authority figures. But that idea of respect was more often about obedience than honouring others. This created an imbalance, as respect was not expected to flow both ways. Unfortunately, under that dynamic, people misused their power. The understanding of respect had to change because obeying someone just because of their position can leave us vulnerable to abuse if that person is acting with ill intent.

People are still learning what it means to treat each other with actual respect — to honour others, to value their existence. It's as if, as a society, we threw out the notion of respect instead of fine-tuning our expectations. The kind of respect we seek as humans is to be acknowledged, seen and heard because we exist. We simply want to be treated with courtesy and consideration. This isn't an unreasonable request. As a society, we need to redefine our concepts of respect so we can model ways to value each other's existence. You have a role to play in this. When you treat others with respect, it demonstrates how they can treat you. This has a ripple effect as humans learn by repetition and role modelling.

Respect is also an inside job. Respect is built on a foundation of worth. It's hard to treat yourself with respect when you don't know you are worthy and don't take care of yourself. You communicate your self-respect to others through how you dress, speak about yourself, manage your finances and look after your belongings. Internally, when you ignore your intuition (signs from your body or emotional cues), you aren't respecting yourself. Self-respect requires you to prize your existence, and by extension, it asks you to be the very best version of yourself that you can be in every moment.

Journal Prompt

In what ways do you disrespect yourself? How do others disrespect you? What steps can you take to value yourself and honour your emotional and physical needs?

Empowered Tapping® Script

Use the following script to work through any fears and trauma associated with your past experiences of respect to create new possibilities. As you tap each of your meridian points, say this script aloud.

I Am Respected

Round 1 (Repeat twice)

TH: Even though it's normal to want to be respected.

EB: My mind can't just let it be normal.

SE: It has to turn it into an unmet need.

UE: This triggers off my fear responses that I will get stuck in my trauma reactions of not being considered.

TL: This then sets off a cascade of emotionally painful and traumatic experiences in my mind's reality.

CH: But it's not how my life really has to be.

CB: It's just my fears running stories from my past.

UB: I don't need certain conditions to exist for me to heal from my experiences of disrespect.

UA: And I don't need specific circumstances to exist for me to transform my fears of not being considered. I already am being respected.

Round 2

TH: By interpreting my need to be respected, being unmet, sets off post-traumatic stress in me I have created a belief that this is how it is and always will be.

EB: That belief that my need to be respected, being unmet, sets off post-traumatic stress in me is how it is and always will be then colours my experiences, so it feels like it's true.

SE: But it's not true.

UE: By interpreting my need to be respected, being unmet, sets off post-traumatic stress in me I have created a belief that this is how it is and always will be.

TL: That belief that my need to be respected, being unmet, sets off post-traumatic stress in me is how it is and always will be then colours my experiences, so it feels like it's true.

CH: But it's not true.

CB: By interpreting my need to be respected, being unmet, sets off post-traumatic stress in me I have created a belief that this is how it is and always will be.

UB: That belief that my need to be respected, being unmet, sets off post-traumatic stress in me is how it is and always will be then colours my experiences, so it feels like it's true.

UA: But it's not true.

Round 3

TH: By interpreting my fear of not being considered as an expression of post-traumatic stress I have created a belief that this is how it is and always will be.

EB: That belief that my fear of not being considered as an expression of post-traumatic stress is how it is and always will be then colours my experiences, so it feels like it's true.

SE: But it's not true.

UE: By interpreting my fear of not being considered as an expression of post-traumatic stress I have created a belief that this is how it is and always will be.

TL: That belief that my fear of not being considered as an expression of post-traumatic stress is how it is and always will be then colours my experiences, so it feels like it's true.

CH: But it's not true.

CB: By interpreting my fear of not being considered as an expression of post-traumatic stress I have created a belief that this is how it is and always will be.

UB: That belief that my fear of not being considered as an expression of post-traumatic stress is how it is and always will be then colours my experiences, so it feels like it's true.

UA: But it's not true.

Round 4

All points: I'm letting it all go.

Round 5

TH: The only truth is I already am being respected.

All remaining points: I already am being respected.

Cycle 19. Nurtured/Attention Withheld

You have the need to be nurtured, and when this need is not met, you feel like others are withholding attention from you. Your fear of attention being withheld drives you to find ways to be nurtured.

Life is filled with complex interactions around nurturing. At points in your life, you will have experiences of feeling neglected by others, and you will create the experience of withheld attention for others. You will perceive the withholding of attention, even when that is not the intention of others, and you will neglect yourself. Your task right now is to identify where this is happening so you can heal the imbalance and align yourself with your true nature.

Being and feeling nurtured is a deeply personal experience. You learnt about this feeling from your mother or primary caregiver in the first year of life when the experience could *only* come from an external source. The attention given in response to your cries, recognising that you communicated your needs through different cries, reinforced your worth and that you were wanted. Where this did not happen, your capacity to receive sustenance and nourishment and to believe your needs could be met was impacted. The depth of being denied permeates throughout your life. You question whether others ever think about you and how you might feel.

As Kelly Clarkson sang in *Where Is Your Heart*, "I don't expect the world to move underneath me, but for God's sake, could you try?" You just want someone to notice you – to give you some attention. When you feel external nurture is denied, you internalise it and don't nurture yourself. Addictions may fill the gap as a substitute for the unmet need. The dopamine release tricks you into feeling better for a time, but it never lasts. You need more and more of whatever you use as a replacement for your need to be nurtured, loved, wanted or worthy. You may consume cake, chocolate, cigarettes, wine, beer, online gaming or gamble to placate your sense of being denied. But, these replacements will never bring you closer to feeling truly nurtured. Deep within, a cry for help is begging you to take care of yourself — to nurture you. Take steps to feed your mind and body what they really need to be at your best.

Journal Prompt

What are you using to fill the gap inside you? What steps can you take to replace addiction with true self-care?

Empowered Tapping® Script

Use the following script to work through any fears and trauma associated with your past experiences of nurturing to create new possibilities. As you tap each of your meridian points, say this script aloud.

I Feel Nurtured

Round 1 (Repeat twice)

TH: Even though it's normal to want to be nurtured.

EB: My mind can't just let it be normal.

SE: It has to turn it into an unmet need.

UE: This triggers off my fear responses that I will get stuck in my trauma reactions of feeling others are withholding attention from me.

TL: This then sets off a cascade of emotionally painful and traumatic experiences in my mind's reality.

CH: But it's not how my life really has to be.

CB: It's just my fears running stories from my past.

UB: I don't need certain conditions to exist for me to heal from my experiences of malnourishment.

UA: And I don't need specific circumstances to exist for me to transform my fears of others withholding attention from me. I already am receiving the attention needed to feel nurtured.

Round 2

TH: By interpreting my need to be nurtured, being unmet, sets off post-traumatic stress in me I have created a belief that this is how it is and always will be.

EB: That belief that my need to be nurturing, being unmet, sets off post-traumatic stress in me is how it is and always will be then colours my experiences, so it feels like it's true.

SE: But it's not true.

UE: By interpreting my need to be nurtured, being unmet, sets off post-traumatic stress in me I have created a belief that this is how it is and always will be.

TL: That belief that my need to be nurturing, being unmet, sets off post-traumatic stress in me is how it is and always will be then colours my experiences, so it feels like it's true.

CH: But it's not true.

CB: By interpreting my need to be nurtured, being unmet, sets off post-traumatic stress in me I have created a belief that this is how it is and always will be.

UB: That belief that my need to be nurturing, being unmet, sets off post-traumatic stress in me is how it is and always will be then colours my experiences, so it feels like it's true.

UA: But it's not true.

Round 3

TH: By interpreting my fear others are withholding attention from me as an expression of post-traumatic stress I have created a belief that this is how it is and always will be.

EB: That belief that my fear others are withholding attention from me as an expression of post-traumatic stress is how it is and always will be then colours my experiences, so it feels like it's true.

SE: But it's not true.

UE: By interpreting my fear others are withholding attention from me as an expression of post-traumatic stress I have created a belief that this is how it is and always will be.

TL: That belief that my fear others are withholding attention from me as an expression of post-traumatic stress is how it is and always will be then colours my experiences, so it feels like it's true.

CH: But it's not true.

CB: By interpreting my fear others are withholding attention from me as an expression of post-traumatic stress I have created a belief that this is how it is and always will be.

UB: That belief that my fear others are withholding attention from me as an expression of post-traumatic stress is how it is and always will be then colours my experiences, so it feels like it's true.

UA: But it's not true.

Round 4

All points: I'm letting it all go.

Round 5

TH: The only truth is I already am receiving the attention needed to feel nurtured.

All remaining points: I already am receiving the attention needed to feel nurtured.

Cycle 20. Supported/Vulnerable

You have the need to be supported, and when this need is not met, you feel vulnerable. Your fear of vulnerability drives you to find ways to be supported.

Life is filled with complex interactions around support. At points in your life, you will have experiences of feeling unsupported by others, and you will create the experience of vulnerability for others. You will perceive vulnerability, even when it is not the intention of others, and you will get stuck in your fear of vulnerability and not support yourself. Your task right now is to identify where this is happening so you can heal the imbalance and align yourself with your true nature.

This core need initially forms between the ages of ten months and two years. Your ability to trust, ask for and receive help, and feel you are believed in influences how you cope with feeling vulnerable. Two drives are created in response to vulnerability. One is to find ways to be supported by others. The other is to push away support by committing to not needing anything or anyone. No one teaches you how to stay present and keep going while feeling vulnerable. This skill comes from your sense of how you were supported, loved and respected in your most vulnerable years, when you needed someone else to take care of everything from feeding and dressing you to soothing your fears and insecurities. Your ability to manage vulnerability stems from the inner security that was provided to you by an outside source. With this security in place, you could encounter the outside world with confidence.

As you grow up, you have to take actions that support the best in you. If you didn't start with the kind of support that helped you manage your vulnerability, you can learn this skill later in life. You can respect yourself and build your sense of security, surety and inner stability to gain a knowing that you are supported, whatever comes your way. Whether you have been needy, desperate, co-dependent or invulnerable, having no needs or wants of your own, you can heal those wounds and learn to support yourself. As you do, people will come into your life who will support you as well. You are not an island. Part of being human is the interdependency that comes from loving and belonging to others as friends or family centred in your own strength.

Journal Prompt

What is your relationship with vulnerability like? Do you end up in the needy-dependent camp or the invulnerable-leave-me-alone camp? Do you swing between the two, depending on the circumstances? What are those circumstances?

Empowered Tapping® Script

Use the following script to work through any fears and trauma associated with your past experiences of support to create new possibilities. As you tap each of your meridian points, say this script aloud.

I Am Supported

Round 1 (Repeat twice)

TH: Even though it's normal to want to be supported.

EB: My mind can't just let it be normal.

SE: It has to turn it into an unmet need.

UE: This triggers off my fear responses that I will get stuck in my trauma reactions of vulnerability.

TL: This then sets off a cascade of emotionally painful and traumatic experiences in my mind's reality.

CH: But it's not how my life really has to be.

CB: It's just my fears running stories from my past.

UB: I don't need certain conditions to exist for me to heal from my experiences of being unsupported.

UA: And I don't need specific circumstances to exist for me to transform my fears of vulnerability. I already am accepting the support offered to me.

Round 2

TH: By interpreting my need to be supported, being unmet, sets off post-traumatic stress in me I have created a belief that this is how it is and always will be.

EB: That belief that my need to be supported, being unmet, sets off post-traumatic stress in me is how it is and always will be then colours my experiences, so it feels like it's true.

SE: But it's not true.

UE: By interpreting my need to be supported, being unmet, sets off post-traumatic stress in me I have created a belief that this is how it is and always will be.

TL: That belief that my need to be supported, being unmet, sets off post-traumatic stress in me is how it is and always will be then colours my experiences, so it feels like it's true.

CH: But it's not true.

CB: By interpreting my need to be supported, being unmet, sets off post-traumatic stress in me I have created a belief that this is how it is and always will be.

UB: That belief that my need to be supported, being unmet, sets off post-traumatic stress in me is how it is and always will be then colours my experiences, so it feels like it's true.

UA: But it's not true.

Round 3

TH: By interpreting my fear of vulnerability as an expression of post-traumatic stress I have created a belief that this is how it is and always will be.

EB: That belief that my fear of vulnerability as an expression of post-traumatic stress is how it is and always will be then colours my experiences, so it feels like it's true.

SE: But it's not true.

UE: By interpreting my fear of vulnerability as an expression of post-traumatic stress I have created a belief that this is how it is and always will be.

TL: That belief that my fear of vulnerability as an expression of post-traumatic stress is how it is and always will be then colours my experiences, so it feels like it's true.

CH: But it's not true.

CB: By interpreting my fear of vulnerability as an expression of post-traumatic stress I have created a belief that this is how it is and always will be.

UB: That belief that my fear of vulnerability as an expression of post-traumatic stress is how it is and always will be then colours my experiences, so it feels like it's true.

UA: But it's not true.

Round 4

All points: I'm letting it all go.

Round 5

TH: The only truth is I already am accepting the support offered to me.

All remaining points: I already am accepting the support offered to me.

Cycle 21. Important/Ignored

You have the need to feel important, and when this need is not met, you feel ignored. Your fear of being ignored drives you to find ways to feel important.

Life is filled with complex interactions around being important. At points in your life, you will have experiences of feeling ignored by others, and you will create the experience of ignoring others. You will perceive being ignored, even when it is not the intention of others, and you will ignore your internal guidance system. Your task right now is to identify where this is happening so you can heal the imbalance and align yourself with your true nature.

A sense of being important is deeply linked to being useful and needed. You want to play a significant role in someone's life. You want to feel like you matter and that this area of priority in your life can't work without you. When others can and do function without you, it can create a sense of being unimportant or ignored. It can feel like you have been dismissed as irrelevant. This hurts. But the answer doesn't lay outside of yourself. Instead, it comes from becoming important to you. Begin by learning to listen to your internal guidance system and not ignoring your needs. Decide that you matter enough to yourself and become a priority in your life. Integrity and congruency demand that you start here. Once you radiate the confidence that stems from being important enough that you take care of your needs and respect your emotional self, others will want to know your secrets. This also means that you will give freely to others because you are not coming from an unmet need. No one will have to make you okay because you know your worth and value

Journal Prompt

Where do you want validation about your importance to someone or something? What do you say or act like in your attempts to feel important?

Empowered Tapping® Script

Use the following script to work through any fears and trauma associated with your past experiences of importance to create new possibilities. As you tap each of your meridian points, say this script aloud.

I Am Important

Round 1 (Repeat twice)

TH: Even though it's normal to want to be important.

EB: My mind can't just let it be normal.

SE: It has to turn it into an unmet need.

UE: This triggers off my fear responses that I will get stuck in my trauma reactions of being ignored.

TL: This then sets off a cascade of emotionally painful and traumatic experiences in my mind's reality.

CH: But it's not how my life really has to be.

CB: It's just my fears running stories from my past.

UB: I don't need certain conditions to exist for me to heal from my experiences of being unimportant.

UA: And I don't need specific circumstances to exist for me to transform my fears of being ignored. I already am allowing my importance to be validated.

Round 2

TH: By interpreting my need to be important, being unmet, sets off post-traumatic stress in me I have created a belief that this is how it is and always will be.

EB: That belief that my need to be important, being unmet, sets off post-traumatic stress in me is how it is and always will be then colours my experiences, so it feels like it's true.

SE: But it's not true.

UE: By interpreting my need to be important, being unmet, sets off post-traumatic stress in me I have created a belief that this is how it is and always will be.

TL: That belief that my need to be important, being unmet, sets off post-traumatic stress in me is how it is and always will be then colours my experiences, so it feels like it's true.

CH: But it's not true.

CB: By interpreting my need to be important, being unmet, sets off post-traumatic stress in me I have created a belief that this is how it is and always will be.

UB: That belief that my need to be important, being unmet, sets off post-traumatic stress in me is how it is and always will be then colours my experiences, so it feels like it's true.

UA: But it's not true.

Round 3

TH: By interpreting my fear of being ignored as an expression of post-traumatic stress I have created a belief that this is how it is and always will be.

EB: That belief that my fear of being ignored as an expression of post-traumatic stress is how it is and always will be then colours my experiences, so it feels like it's true.

SE: But it's not true.

UE: By interpreting my fear of being ignored as an expression of post-traumatic stress I have created a belief that this is how it is and always will be.

TL: That belief that my fear of being ignored as an expression of post-traumatic stress is how it is and always will be then colours my experiences, so it feels like it's true.

CH: But it's not true.

CB: By interpreting my fear of being ignored as an expression of post-traumatic stress I have created a belief that this is how it is and always will be.

UB: That belief that my fear of being ignored as an expression of post-traumatic stress is how it is and always will be then colours my experiences, so it feels like it's true.

UA: But it's not true.

Round 4

All points: I'm letting it all go.

Round 5

TH: The only truth is I already am allowing my importance to be validated.

All remaining points: I already am allowing my importance to be validated.

Cycle 22. Trust/Betrayal

You have the need to trust, and when this need is not met, you feel betrayed. Your fear of betrayal drives you to find ways to create a sense of trust.

Life is filled with complex interactions around trust. At points in your life, you will have experiences of feeling betrayed by others, and you will create the experience of betrayal for others. You will perceive betrayal, even when it is not the intention of others, and you will betray yourself. Your task right now is to identify where this is happening so you can heal the imbalance and align yourself with your true nature.

Feeling betrayed by someone tears away your trust. It leaves you feeling like you can't rely on a word they say. And nor should you. They have to prove their trustworthiness to you. They have done the wrong thing. It's on them. Don't make it your responsibility by shrinking or withdrawing your beauty and presence in the world as a method of self-protection. Hold them accountable and set some boundaries and expectations while acknowledging the hurt. Don't turn the hurt into a wound that you wear in the hope they will realise the depth to which they impacted you. The fact that you feel betrayed is all the evidence needed. The relationship has been damaged — now choose to allow it to be healed or walk away. What can you learn from the experience to help you navigate relationships with others in the future?

Trust is vital for a sense of safety. Living in fear of vulnerability, being paranoid and questioning everyone's motives becomes exhausting. If your trust radar is tuned to hypersensitive, you need to heal old hurts and reset your sensor. It is so easy and natural to internalise your experiences of betrayal and end up not trusting your life processes. Betraying yourself is even more painful. Filter your decisions, interpretations and perceptions through a clear lens. If you don't trust yourself, the Universe/God or anyone else, how can you move through your life with flow, ease and joy? You will feel tense, on edge, hypervigilant and wary. It's draining to live like this. Your energetic resources will be limited, and your physical health compromised. Trust must be earned. Never give it away. It does take a willingness to be vulnerable, but when you surrender a little to your divine plan, you can build confidence in it. Step by step, you will come to trust that the Universe/God has your best interests at heart, and magic will happen.

Journal Prompt

What state is your trust bucket in? How well can you navigate life and relationships based on the amount of trust you are carrying with you?

Empowered Tapping® Script

Use the following script to work through any fears and trauma associated with your past experiences of trust to create new possibilities. As you tap each of your meridian points, say this script aloud.

I Decipher Who I Trust

Round 1 (Repeat twice)

TH: Even though it's normal to want to trust others.

EB: My mind can't just let it be normal.

SE: It has to turn it into an unmet need.

UE: This triggers off my fear responses that I will get stuck in my trauma reactions of being betrayed.

TL: This then sets off a cascade of emotionally painful and traumatic experiences in my mind's reality.

CH: But it's not how my life really has to be.

CB: It's just my fears running stories from my past.

UB: I don't need certain conditions to exist for me to heal from my experiences of untrustworthiness.

UA: And I don't need specific circumstances to exist for me to transform my fears of betrayal. I already am deciphering who is trustworthy.

Round 2

TH: By interpreting my need to trust others, being unmet, sets off post-traumatic stress in me I have created a belief that this is how it is and always will be.

EB: That belief that my need to trust others, being unmet, sets off post-traumatic stress in me is how it is and always will be then colours my experiences, so it feels like it's true.

SE: But it's not true.

UE: By interpreting my need to trust others, being unmet, sets off post-traumatic stress in me I have created a belief that this is how it is and always will be.

TL: That belief that my need to trust others, being unmet, sets off post-traumatic stress in me is how it is and always will be then colours my experiences, so it feels like it's true.

CH: But it's not true.

CB: By interpreting my need to trust others, being unmet, sets off post-traumatic stress in me I have created a belief that this is how it is and always will be.

UB: That belief that my need to trust others, being unmet, sets off post-traumatic stress in me is how it is and always will be then colours my experiences, so it feels like it's true.

UA: But it's not true.

Round 3

TH: By interpreting my fear of being betrayed as an expression of post-traumatic stress I have created a belief that this is how it is and always will be.

EB: That belief that my fear of being betrayed as an expression of post-traumatic stress is how it is and always will be then colours my experiences, so it feels like it's true.

SE: But it's not true.

UE: By interpreting my fear of being betrayed as an expression of post-traumatic stress I have created a belief that this is how it is and always will be.

TL: That belief that my fear of being betrayed as an expression of post-traumatic stress is how it is and always will be then colours my experiences, so it feels like it's true.

CH: But it's not true.

CB: By interpreting my fear of being betrayed as an expression of post-traumatic stress I have created a belief that this is how it is and always will be.

UB: That belief that my fear of being betrayed as an expression of post-traumatic stress is how it is and always will be then colours my experiences, so it feels like it's true.

UA: But it's not true.

Round 4

All points: I'm letting it all go.

Round 5

TH: The only truth is I already am deciphering who is trustworthy.

All remaining points: I already am deciphering who is trustworthy.

Cycle 23. Understood/Compassion Withheld

You have the need to be understood, and when this need is not met, you feel compassion is being withheld. Your fear of compassion being withheld drives you to find ways to be understood.

Life is filled with complex interactions around being understood. At points in your life, you will experience compassion being withheld by others, and you will create the experience of withholding compassion for others. You will perceive compassion being withheld, even when it is not the intention of others, and you will withhold compassion from yourself. Your task right now is to identify where this is happening so you can heal the imbalance and align yourself with your true nature.

In *The 7 Habits of Highly Effective People*, Stephen R. Covey says: "Seek first to understand, then to be understood." The challenge comes in wanting to be understood first. When you feel compassion is being withheld, it's natural to want to be understood, often desperately. The intensity of the need stems from the inner sense of being punished. When others don't understand your experiences or perspectives, their responses often feel punitive. It's easy to become stuck in feeling punished and defensive, but it doesn't change the relationship dynamics. Understanding is the remedy. Likewise, you can lack compassion for yourself because of misinterpretations you have made about a particular situation.

It is time we learn how to effectively manage our emotions collectively. It is likely that you weren't raised to know how to use your internal guidance system, that all emotions have a purpose and that they tell you how you are experiencing life. When you listen to the personal meaning of your interpretation of the scenarios you face, you can work through 95-98% of the repeating mental chatter that regurgitates your past. By identifying the purpose of a feeling, you can understand yourself better and, by extension, have a greater sense of compassion for yourself. From this act of self-kindness, you will feel more able to overcome any obstacle before you.

Journal Prompt

Write your own emotional manual. Detail your emotions and the messages they bring to your awareness.

Empowered Tapping® Script

You can use the following script to work through any fears and trauma associated with your past experiences of being understood to create new possibilities. As you tap each of your meridian points, say this script aloud.

I Am Understood

Round 1 (Repeat twice)

TH: Even though it's normal to want to be understood.

EB: My mind can't just let it be normal.

SE: It has to turn it into an unmet need.

UE: This triggers off my fear responses that I will get stuck in my trauma reactions of feeling compassion is being withheld.

TL: This then sets off a cascade of emotionally painful and traumatic experiences in my mind's reality.

CH: But it's not how my life really has to be.

CB: It's just my fears running stories from my past.

UB: I don't need certain conditions to exist for me to heal from my experiences of being misunderstood.

UA: And I don't need specific circumstances to exist for me to transform my fears of compassion being withheld. I already am understood.

Round 2

TH: By interpreting my need to be understood, being unmet, sets off post-traumatic stress in me I have created a belief that this is how it is and always will be.

EB: That belief that my need to be understood, being unmet, sets off post-traumatic stress in me is how it is and always will be then colours my experiences, so it feels like it's true.

SE: But it's not true.

UE: By interpreting my need to be understood, being unmet, sets off post-traumatic stress in me I have created a belief that this is how it is and always will be.

TL: That belief that my need to be understood, being unmet, sets off post-traumatic stress in me is how it is and always will be then colours my experiences, so it feels like it's true.

CH: But it's not true.

CB: By interpreting my need to be understood, being unmet, sets off post-traumatic stress in me I have created a belief that this is how it is and always will be.

UB: That belief that my need to be understood, being unmet, sets off post-traumatic stress in me is how it is and always will be then colours my experiences, so it feels like it's true.

UA: But it's not true.

Round 3

TH: By interpreting my fear of compassion being withheld as an expression of post-traumatic stress I have created a belief that this is how it is and always will be.

EB: That belief that my fear of compassion being withheld as an expression of post-traumatic stress is how it is and always will be then colours my experiences, so it feels like it's true.

SE: But it's not true.

UE: By interpreting my fear of compassion being withheld as an expression of post-traumatic stress I have created a belief that this is how it is and always will be.

TL: That belief that my fear of compassion being withheld as an expression of post-traumatic stress is how it is and always will be then colours my experiences, so it feels like it's true.

CH: But it's not true.

CB: By interpreting my fear of compassion being withheld as an expression of post-traumatic stress I have created a belief that this is how it is and always will be.

UB: That belief that my fear of compassion being withheld as an expression of post-traumatic stress is how it is and always will be then colours my experiences, so it feels like it's true.

UA: But it's not true.

Round 4

All points: I'm letting it all go.

Round 5

TH: The only truth is l already am understood.

All remaining points: I already am understood.

Cycle 24. Connected/Disconnected

You have the need to feel connected, and when this need is not met, you feel disconnected. Your fear of disconnection drives you to find ways to feel connected.

Life is filled with complex interactions around connection. At points in your life, you will have experiences of feeling disconnected from others, and you will create the experience of disconnection for others. You will perceive disconnection, even when it is not the intention of others, and you will disconnect from yourself. Your task right now is to identify where this is happening so you can heal the imbalance and align yourself with your true nature.

The desire for connection is found in the wiring of your brain. This desire for safety is strongly linked to the need to belong and for support. But connection brings the flavour of closeness and nourishment to your life. As life becomes more digitised, it reduces the experience of human interaction and touch. You no longer catch up with friends in person but jump online and send a message through the numerous chat apps available. Instead of going into the bank or supermarket, you can jump online and shop to your heart's content. Whatever you purchase is then delivered to your door, and you may not have to talk to a single person throughout the entire process.

Our world is becoming disconnected from human interaction. As a result, you may feel disconnected from the key elements provided by physical touch, such as looking into the eyes of a friend, hearing the soothing tone of a calming, loving voice, smelling the pheromones that set off desire and tasting the joys of a shared meal. After two years of almost no physical time in classrooms in Victoria, Australia, teachers were confronted with re-educating children on how to socialise and behave in a class setting. Kids had become disconnected from human interactions. Left to their own devices, they had lost the ability to relate to others in socially respectful ways. Likewise, you can disconnect from your inner world of intuition and feelings. You can stop listening to the messages from your body about what it needs and what it doesn't. Your mind can be *so* in control that you are robotic in your engagement with life. You can forget how to nourish your soul, nurture your spirit, honour your feelings and respect your body. Connecting with yourself is as important as connecting with the world around you — humans, animals and nature.

The world doesn't have to stay this disconnected, and neither do you. Choose to nourish yourself and your relationships by connecting to your inner and outer worlds and set your senses on fire with delight and wonder in the magic surrounding you.

Journal Prompt

Make a list of the things that delight you each day. Now make them real, do them. Listen to your body talk to you. What is it saying?

Empowered Tapping® Script

Use the following script to work through any fears and trauma associated with your past experiences of connection to create new possibilities. As you tap each of your meridian points, say this script aloud.

I Am Connected

Round 1 (Repeat twice)

TH: Even though it's normal to want a deep connection.

EB: My mind can't just let it be normal.

SE: It has to turn it into an unmet need.

UE: This triggers off my fear responses that I will get stuck in my trauma reactions of disconnection.

TL: This then sets off a cascade of emotionally painful and traumatic experiences in my mind's reality.

CH: But it's not how my life really has to be.

CB: It's just my fears running stories from my past.

UB: I don't need certain conditions to exist for me to heal from my experiences of lacking connection.

UA: And I don't need specific circumstances to exist for me to transform my fears of disconnection. I already am deeply connected.

Round 2

TH: By interpreting my need to deeply connect, being unmet, sets off post-traumatic stress in me I have created a belief that this is how it is and always will be.

EB: That belief that my need to deeply connect, being unmet, sets off post-traumatic stress in me is how it is and always will be then colours my experiences, so it feels like it's true.

SE: But it's not true.

UE: By interpreting my need to deeply connect, being unmet, sets off post-traumatic stress in me I have created a belief that this is how it is and always will be.

TL: That belief that my need to deeply connect, being unmet, sets off post-traumatic stress in me is how it is and always will be then colours my experiences, so it feels like it's true.

CH: But it's not true.

CB: By interpreting my need to deeply connect, being unmet, sets off post-traumatic stress in me I have created a belief that this is how it is and always will be.

UB: That belief that my need to deeply connect, being unmet, sets off post-traumatic stress in me is how it is and always will be then colours my experiences, so it feels like it's true.

UA: But it's not true.

Round 3

TH: By interpreting my fear of disconnection as an expression of post-traumatic stress I have created a belief that this is how it is and always will be.

EB: That belief that my fear of disconnection as an expression of post-traumatic stress is how it is and always will be then colours my experiences, so it feels like it's true.

SE: But it's not true.

UE: By interpreting my fear of disconnection as an expression of post-traumatic stress I have created a belief that this is how it is and always will be.

TL: That belief that my fear of disconnection as an expression of post-traumatic stress is how it is and always will be then colours my experiences, so it feels like it's true.

CH: But it's not true.

CB: By interpreting my fear of disconnection as an expression of post-traumatic stress I have created a belief that this is how it is and always will be.

UB: That belief that my fear of disconnection as an expression of post-traumatic stress is how it is and always will be then colours my experiences, so it feels like it's true.

UA: But it's not true.

Round 4

All points: I'm letting it all go.

ROUND 5

TH: The only truth is I already am deeply connected.

All remaining points: I already am deeply connected.

Cycle 25. Authentic/Imperfection

You have the need to be authentic, and when this need is not met, you feel imperfect. Your fear of imperfection drives you to find ways to be authentic.

Life is filled with complex interactions around authenticity. At points in your life, you will have experiences of feeling imperfect to others, and you will create the experience of imperfection for others. You will perceive being flawed, even when it is not the intention of others, and you will judge yourself as imperfect. Your task right now is to identify where this is happening so you can heal the imbalance and align yourself with your true nature.

The world is moving through a paradigm shift from perfection to authenticity. For generations, people were raised to believe they had to be perfect. You could only be loved when you were perfect. You were good enough once you were perfect. You deserved your dreams to come true when you were perfect. Until then, you were imperfect and needed the approval of others to make you okay. But, of course, perfection doesn't really exist. It's an ideal, a standard or expectation that someone makes up and demands you to live by or meet. As the cloak has been removed from the falsity of perfection, new language describes what you are to seek, and that is authenticity. Aim to be who you are. To be real. To shine your uniqueness for all to see. Now, you are under pressure to be different while finding a new group of people who share your differences. Society has dissected our identities and turned the normal processes of growing up and questioning who we are into a business. Being offended by anyone who doesn't understand or embrace your displays of individuality is the new norm. But none of this brings you any closer to being authentic, even if society tells you it is.

Being authentic is a quiet event. It is an acceptance of yourself without fanfare. It is a deep knowing of who you are, what you value and what you believe in based on your experiences and personality. Authenticity is about being true to yourself while allowing others to be true to themselves. It is done with love, empathy and compassion for all.

Journal Prompt

How has perfectionism impacted your life? Who is the authentic you?

Empowered Tapping® Script

Use the following script to work through any fears and trauma associated with your past experiences of authenticity to create new possibilities. As you tap each of your meridian points, say this script aloud.

I Accept My Authenticity

Round 1 (Repeat twice)

TH: Even though it's normal to want to be authentic.

EB: My mind can't just let it be normal.

SE: It has to turn it into an unmet need.

UE: This triggers off my fear responses that I will get stuck in my trauma reactions of feeling imperfect and flawed.

TL: This then sets off a cascade of emotionally painful and traumatic experiences in my mind's reality.

CH: But it's not how my life really has to be.

CB: It's just my fears running stories from my past.

UB: I don't need certain conditions to exist for me to heal from my experiences of inauthentic words, behaviours and actions.

UA: And I don't need specific circumstances to exist for me to transform my fears of feeling imperfect and flawed. I already am accepting my authenticity.

Round 2

TH: By interpreting my need to be authentic, being unmet, sets off post-traumatic stress in me I have created a belief that this is how it is and always will be.

EB: That belief that my need to be authentic, being unmet, sets off post-traumatic stress in me is how it is and always will be then colours my experiences, so it feels like it's true.

SE: But it's not true.

UE: By interpreting my need to be authentic, being unmet, sets off post-traumatic stress in me I have created a belief that this is how it is and always will be.

TL: That belief that my need to be authentic, being unmet, sets off post-traumatic stress in me is how it is and always will be then colours my experiences, so it feels like it's true.

CH: But it's not true.

CB: By interpreting my need to be authentic, being unmet, sets off post-traumatic stress in me I have created a belief that this is how it is and always will be.

UB: That belief that my need to be authentic, being unmet, sets off post-traumatic stress in me is how it is and always will be then colours my experiences, so it feels like it's true.

UA: But it's not true.

Round 3

TH: By interpreting my fear of imperfection as an expression of post-traumatic stress I have created a belief that this is how it is and always will be.

EB: That belief that my fear of imperfection as an expression of post-traumatic stress is how it is and always will be then colours my experiences, so it feels like it's true.

SE: But it's not true.

UE: By interpreting my fear of imperfection as an expression of post-traumatic stress I have created a belief that this is how it is and always will be.

TL: That belief that my fear of imperfection as an expression of post-traumatic stress is how it is and always will be then colours my experiences, so it feels like it's true.

CH: But it's not true.

CB: By interpreting my fear of imperfection as an expression of post-traumatic stress I have created a belief that this is how it is and always will be.

UB: That belief that my fear of imperfection as an expression of post-traumatic stress is how it is and always will be then colours my experiences, so it feels like it's true.

UA: But it's not true.

Round 4

All points: I'm letting it all go.

Round 5

TH: The only truth is I already am accepting my authenticity.

All remaining points: I already am accepting my authenticity.

Cycle 26. Adored/Care Withheld

You have the need to feel adored, and when this need is not met, you feel as if care is being withheld from you. Your fear of care being withheld drives you to find ways to be adored.

Life is filled with complex interactions around adoration. At points in your life, you will have experiences of feeling care being withheld by others, and you will create the experience of withholding care for others. You will perceive care being withheld, even when it is not the intention of others, and you will withhold care from yourself. Your task right now is to identify where this is happening so you can heal the imbalance and align yourself with your true nature.

It is so easy to feel like people don't care about you. How often, in modern society, do you hear expressions such as, "I don't care," or "who cares?" or "I couldn't care less"? You may even hear that what you want or how you feel won't change what is happening. Of course, no one really doesn't care about you unless they are being selfish and self-centred. It's just an expression of frustration, defiance or control. But that doesn't stop it hurting when someone says they *don't care*. In that moment, you want to be adored and cared about. But you can't let words said in frustration or to minimise you, define your worth. Be brave and respond by asking them, "So you really don't care about me?" If they reply that they don't, you will have learnt a lot about your relationship with them.

Then, there is the relationship you have with yourself. Self-care is an act of love. Acknowledging what makes you lovable helps you attract a respectful and adoring partner. When you don't hold space for your unique qualities and know you are adorable, you will feel vulnerable to the opinions of others. When you embrace your adorability, your presence vibrates with an energy that draws people to you through your inner confidence. With authenticity, you radiate a warm and accepting charisma of what is adorable in others because you feel secure within.

Journal Prompt

Who do you adore? What is it about them that you adore? Who adores you? What is adorable about you?

Empowered Tapping® Script

Use the following script to work through any fears and trauma associated with your past experiences of adoration to create new possibilities. As you tap each of your meridian points, say this script aloud.

I Am Adored

Round 1 (Repeat twice)

TH: Even though it's normal to want to be adored.

EB: My mind can't just let it be normal.

SE: It has to turn it into an unmet need.

UE: This triggers off my fear responses that I will get stuck in my trauma reactions of feeling as if care is being withheld.

TL: This then sets off a cascade of emotionally painful and traumatic experiences in my mind's reality.

CH: But it's not how my life really has to be.

CB: It's just my fears running stories from my past.

UB: I don't need certain conditions to exist for me to heal from my experiences of not being adored.

UA: And I don't need specific circumstances to exist for me to transform my fears of care being withheld. I already am feeling adored.

Round 2

TH: By interpreting my need to be adored, being unmet, sets off post-traumatic stress in me I have created a belief that this is how it is and always will be.

EB: That belief that my need to be adored, being unmet, sets off post-traumatic stress in me is how it is and always will be then colours my experiences, so it feels like it's true.

SE: But it's not true.

UE: By interpreting my need to be adored, being unmet, sets off post-traumatic stress in me I have created a belief that this is how it is and always will be.

TL: That belief that my need to be adored, being unmet, sets off post-traumatic stress in me is how it is and always will be then colours my experiences, so it feels like it's true.

CH: But it's not true.

CB: By interpreting my need to be adored, being unmet, sets off post-traumatic stress in me I have created a belief that this is how it is and always will be.

UB: That belief that my need to be adored, being unmet, sets off post-traumatic stress in me is how it is and always will be then colours my experiences, so it feels like it's true.

UA: But it's not true.

Round 3

TH: By interpreting my fear of care being withheld as an expression of post-traumatic stress I have created a belief that this is how it is and always will be.

EB: That belief that my fear of care being withheld as an expression of post-traumatic stress is how it is and always will be then colours my experiences, so it feels like it's true.

SE: But it's not true.

UE: By interpreting my fear of care being withheld as an expression of post-traumatic stress I have created a belief that this is how it is and always will be.

TL: That belief that my fear of care being withheld as an expression of post-traumatic stress is how it is and always will be then colours my experiences, so it feels like it's true.

CH: But it's not true.

CB: By interpreting my fear of care being withheld as an expression of post-traumatic stress I have created a belief that this is how it is and always will be.

UB: That belief that my fear of care being withheld as an expression of post-traumatic stress is how it is and always will be then colours my experiences, so it feels like it's true.

UA: But it's not true.

Round 4

All points: I'm letting it all go.

Round 5

TH: The only truth is I already am feeling adored.

All remaining points: I already am feeling adored.

Cycle 27. Special/Love Withheld

You have the need to feel special, and when this need is not met, you feel as if love is being withheld. Your fear of love being withheld drives you to find ways to feel special.

Life is filled with complex interactions around feeling special. At points in your life, you will have experiences of feeling love being withheld by others, and you will create the experience of withholding love for others. You will perceive love being withheld, even when it is not the intention of others, and you will withhold love from yourself. Your task right now is to identify where this is happening so you can heal the imbalance and align yourself with your true nature.

Here's the thing – *you are special.* However, you are also not *so special* that you are better or more important than anyone else. Holding a space where this is true, you are then looking for love in the actions, words and behaviours of others and, of course, yourself to validate your specialness. In his book, *The 5 Love Languages,* Gary Chapman wrote that when your love languages aren't met, you feel like you aren't loved. Moreover, you believe people are intentionally withholding love from you. But don't forget, people display love in the way they want to be loved. This means that if your love language consists of *words of affirmation* and *quality time,* but a partner has the love languages of *gift-giving and physical touch,* not only will you not feel loved by their actions, but they won't feel loved by yours. This will result in the need to feel special being unmet for both parties.

There is also what you do to yourself. Self-punishment is withholding love from yourself. What makes you think you warrant how you treat yourself? When you place conditions on love and use it as a weapon, it's no longer love. Instead, it is an act of spite, jealousy, envy, hatred, insecurity, shame, anger, self-doubt, defensiveness, hostility, frustration, irritation, annoyance, selfishness, lust, power, domination, inadequacy or any other less-than-nurturing emotion or desire you wish to think of. Is this how you want to continue to treat yourself or anyone else? Identify what makes you feel loved and embrace that you are special without the flashing lights. You can then relax into enjoying being yourself while enjoying others for who they are.

Journal Prompt

What makes you feel special? How do you express and want to be shown love?

Empowered Tapping® Script

Use the following script to work through any fears and trauma associated with your past experiences of being special to create new possibilities. As you tap each of your meridian points, say this script aloud.

I Accept My Specialness

Round 1 (Repeat twice)

TH: Even though it's normal to want to feel special.

EB: My mind can't just let it be normal.

SE: It has to turn it into an unmet need.

UE: This triggers off my fear responses that I will get stuck in my trauma reactions of feeling like love is being withheld from me.

TL: This then sets off a cascade of emotionally painful and traumatic experiences in my mind's reality.

CH: But it's not how my life really has to be.

CB: It's just my fears running stories from my past.

UB: I don't need certain conditions to exist for me to heal from my experiences of not feeling special.

UA: And I don't need specific circumstances to exist for me to transform my fears of love being withheld. I already am accepting my specialness.

Round 2

TH: By interpreting my need to feel special, being unmet, sets off post-traumatic stress in me I have created a belief that this is how it is and always will be.

EB: That belief that my need to feel special, being unmet, sets off post-traumatic stress in me is how it is and always will be then colours my experiences, so it feels like it's true.

SE: But it's not true.

UE: By interpreting my need to feel special, being unmet, sets off post-traumatic stress in me I have created a belief that this is how it is and always will be.

TL: That belief that my need to feel special, being unmet, sets off post-traumatic stress in me is how it is and always will be then colours my experiences, so it feels like it's true.

CH: But it's not true.

CB: By interpreting my need to feel special, being unmet, sets off post-traumatic stress in me I have created a belief that this is how it is and always will be.

UB: That belief that my need to feel special, being unmet, sets off post-traumatic stress in me is how it is and always will be then colours my experiences, so it feels like it's true.

UA: But it's not true.

Round 3

TH: By interpreting my fear of love being withheld as an expression of post-traumatic stress I have created a belief that this is how it is and always will be.

EB: That belief that my fear of love being withheld as an expression of post-traumatic stress is how it is and always will be then colours my experiences, so it feels like it's true.

SE: But it's not true.

UE: By interpreting my fear of love being withheld as an expression of post-traumatic stress I have created a belief that this is how it is and always will be.

TL: That belief that my fear of love being withheld as an expression of post-traumatic stress is how it is and always will be then colours my experiences, so it feels like it's true.

CH: But it's not true.

CB: By interpreting my fear of love being withheld as an expression of post-traumatic stress I have created a belief that this is how it is and always will be.

UB: That belief that my fear of love being withheld as an expression of post-traumatic stress is how it is and always will be then colours my experiences, so it feels like it's true.

UA: But it's not true.

Round 4

All points: I'm letting it all go.

Round 5

TH: The only truth is I already am accepting my specialness.

All remaining points: I already am accepting my specialness.

Cycle 28. Admired/Interest Withheld

You have the need to be admired, and when this need is not met, you feel as if interest in you is being withheld. Your fear of interest being withheld drives you to find ways to be admired.

Life is filled with complex interactions around being admired. At points in your life, you will have experiences of feeling interest being withheld by others, and you will create the experience of withholding interest for others. You will perceive interest being withheld, even when it is not the intention of others, and you will withhold interest in yourself. Your task right now is to identify where this is happening so you can heal the imbalance and align yourself with your true nature.

In a world that doesn't want you to have a big ego, it's hard to accept the want to be admired. This is especially true when admiration seems to be reserved for the famous and exceptional. Yet, the need persists because you want to feel like someone is interested in you and that you are interesting. While your achievements, skills, abilities, talents, gifts or even your sense of self-assurance or satisfaction don't need to be in neon lights, it's nice to get a pat on the back from someone. It's also important to pause long enough to recognise your own processes and feel a sense of self-satisfaction. When you don't self-assess, self-evaluate and acknowledge your skills, abilities and growth, you maintain a lack of confidence in yourself. This keeps you focused on external sources for reassurance and approval. While your source of admiration remains outside yourself, you keep suffering, stay powerless and feel like a victim. You are relevant, and your experiences are yours. How you live, trying to make sense of everything and reconnect with who you have always been, is admirable. Keep going!

Journal Prompt

What does someone need to do or say before you to feel like they are interested in you? What actions, words or behaviours would tell you that you are someone others could admire? Do you feel that others have confidence in you? Do you have confidence in yourself?

Empowered Tapping® Script

Use the following script to work through any fears and trauma associated with your past experiences of admiration to create new possibilities. As you tap each of your meridian points, say this script aloud.

I Accept Admiration

Round 1 (Repeat twice)

TH: Even though it's normal to want to be admired.

EB: My mind can't just let it be normal.

SE: It has to turn it into an unmet need.

UE: This triggers off my fear responses that I will get stuck in my trauma reactions of feeling as if interest in me is being withheld.

TL: This then sets off a cascade of emotionally painful and traumatic experiences in my mind's reality.

CH: But it's not how my life really has to be.

CB: It's just my fears running stories from my past.

UB: I don't need certain conditions to exist for me to heal from my experiences of not being admired.

UA: And I don't need specific circumstances to exist for me to transform my fears of interest in me being withheld. I already am accepting admiration.

Round 2

TH: By interpreting my need to be admired, being unmet, sets off post-traumatic stress in me I have created a belief that this is how it is and always will be.

EB: That belief that my need to be admired, being unmet, sets off post-traumatic stress in me is how it is and always will be then colours my experiences, so it feels like it's true.

SE: But it's not true.

UE: By interpreting my need to be admired, being unmet, sets off post-traumatic stress in me I have created a belief that this is how it is and always will be.

TL: That belief that my need to be admired, being unmet, sets off post-traumatic stress in me is how it is and always will be then colours my experiences, so it feels like it's true.

CH: But it's not true.

CB: By interpreting my need to be admired, being unmet, sets off post-traumatic stress in me I have created a belief that this is how it is and always will be.

UB: That belief that my need to be admired, being unmet, sets off post-traumatic stress in me is how it is and always will be then colours my experiences, so it feels like it's true.

UA: But it's not true.

Round 3

TH: By interpreting my fear of interest in me being withheld as an expression of post-traumatic stress I have created a belief that this is how it is and always will be.

EB: That belief that my fear of interest in me being withheld as an expression of post-traumatic stress is how it is and always will be then colours my experiences, so it feels like it's true.

SE: But it's not true.

UE: By interpreting my fear of interest in me being withheld as an expression of post-traumatic stress I have created a belief that this is how it is and always will be.

TL: That belief that my fear of interest in me being withheld as an expression of post-traumatic stress is how it is and always will be then colours my experiences, so it feels like it's true.

CH: But it's not true.

CB: By interpreting my fear of interest in me being withheld as an expression of post-traumatic stress I have created a belief that this is how it is and always will be.

UB: That belief that my fear of interest in me being withheld as an expression of post-traumatic stress is how it is and always will be then colours my experiences, so it feels like it's true.

UA: But it's not true.

Round 4

All points: I'm letting it all go.

Round 5

TH: The only truth is I already am accepting admiration.

All remaining points: I already am accepting admiration.

Cycle 29. Cherished/Empathy Withheld

You have the need to feel cherished, and when this need is not met, you feel empathy is being withheld. Your fear of empathy being withheld drives you to find ways to feel cherished.

Life is filled with complex interactions around being cherished. At points in your life, you will have experiences of feeling empathy being withheld by others, and you will create the experience of withholding empathy for others. You will perceive empathy being withheld, even when it is not the intention of others, and you will withhold empathy for yourself. Your task right now is to identify where this is happening so you can heal the imbalance and align yourself with your true nature.

Empathy is the ability to put yourself in another's shoes and see the world as they see it. In other words, empathy is the ability to understand someone based on their beliefs, attitudes, experiences, values and perceptions rather than through your sense of self. When someone empathises with you, you feel cherished, valued and seen. Empathy respects who you are and how you show up in the world. It is a beautiful gift that supports connection and a sense of belonging.

Empathy also applies to yourself. Too often, you will withhold empathy for your own story, your own hurts and your own wounds. Maybe you have confused feeling sorry for yourself with empathy. You may then be stuck in helplessness or hopelessness. Self-pity won't transform your situation, but empathy will. Put yourself in context. What is your conditioning: gendered, societal, religious, generational, familial and cultural? Embrace all of yourself without judgement and condemnation. Be as kind to yourself as you would be to someone else who has been through what you have been through. Cherish the choices you made to survive while recognising that those coping mechanisms are not who you are and may not be serving you any longer. You are more than your experiences and can keep growing and evolving into who you have always been. Holding a space of empathy for yourself makes the journey a little easier.

Journal Prompt

What is your context? Write your story down and read it as if it were someone else's. How would you treat them? What steps can you take to be kinder to yourself?

Empowered Tapping® Script

Use the following script to work through any fears and trauma associated with your past experiences of being cherished to create new possibilities. As you tap each of your meridian points, say this script aloud.

I Am Cherished

Round 1 (Repeat twice)

TH: Even though it's normal to want to be cherished.

EB: My mind can't just let it be normal.

SE: It has to turn it into an unmet need.

UE: This triggers off my fear responses that I will get stuck in my trauma reactions of feeling like empathy is being withheld.

TL: This then sets off a cascade of emotionally painful and traumatic experiences in my mind's reality.

CH: But it's not how my life really has to be.

CB: It's just my fears running stories from my past.

UB: I don't need certain conditions to exist for me to heal from my experiences of not being cherished.

UA: And I don't need specific circumstances to exist for me to transform my fears of empathy being withheld. I already am being cherished.

Round 2

TH: By interpreting my need to be cherished, being unmet, sets off post-traumatic stress in me I have created a belief that this is how it is and always will be.

EB: That belief that my need to be cherished, being unmet, sets off post-traumatic stress in me is how it is and always will be then colours my experiences, so it feels like it's true.

SE: But it's not true.

UE: By interpreting my need to be cherished, being unmet, sets off post-traumatic stress in me I have created a belief that this is how it is and always will be.

TL: That belief that my need to be cherished, being unmet, sets off post-traumatic stress in me is how it is and always will be then colours my experiences, so it feels like it's true.

CH: But it's not true.

CB: By interpreting my need to be cherished, being unmet, sets off post-traumatic stress in me I have created a belief that this is how it is and always will be.

UB: That belief that my need to be cherished, being unmet, sets off post-traumatic stress in me is how it is and always will be then colours my experiences, so it feels like it's true.

UA: But it's not true.

Round 3

TH: By interpreting my fear of empathy being withheld as an expression of post-traumatic stress I have created a belief that this is how it is and always will be.

EB: That belief that my fear of empathy being withheld as an expression of post-traumatic stress is how it is and always will be then colours my experiences, so it feels like it's true.

SE: But it's not true.

UE: By interpreting my fear of empathy being withheld as an expression of post-traumatic stress I have created a belief that this is how it is and always will be.

TL: That belief that my fear of empathy being withheld as an expression of post-traumatic stress is how it is and always will be then colours my experiences, so it feels like it's true.

CH: But it's not true.

CB: By interpreting my fear of empathy being withheld as an expression of post-traumatic stress I have created a belief that this is how it is and always will be.

UB: That belief that my fear of empathy being withheld as an expression of post-traumatic stress is how it is and always will be then colours my experiences, so it feels like it's true.

UA: But it's not true.

Round 4

All points: I'm letting it all go.

Round 5

TH: The only truth is I already am being cherished.

All remaining points: I already am being cherished.

Cycle 30. Reward and Celebration/Punishment

You have the need to be rewarded and celebrated, and when this need is not met, you feel punished. Your fear of punishment drives you to find ways to be rewarded and celebrated.

Life is filled with complex interactions around being rewarded and celebrated. At points in your life, you will have experiences of feeling punished by others, and you will create the experience of punishing others. You will perceive punishment, even when it is not the intention of others, and you will punish yourself. Your task right now is to identify where this is happening so you can heal the imbalance and align yourself with your true nature.

The world is very punitive. You aren't going to get away from that, but you can change how you experience attempts by others to punish you. Your self-punishment can also be explored and transformed. The feeling of being punished usually stems from a sense that you are losing something. What do you fear you are losing? When you are rewarded and celebrated, you feel you are being recognised, seen and valued for a specific quality, trait, talent, skill, ability or accomplishment. What do you expect of yourself and of others? Which of your beliefs contribute to your life feeling punitive? If you expect *everything* to be easy, you build failure into your experiences. If you expect *everything* to be hard, you build struggle into your life. Of course, some things will come with ease, and others will take a lot of work. But where you have created absolutes, limitations, opposites and the shadow, they form and manifest in your life. Yes, the world is punitive, but you don't have to participate in the punishment. Not of yourself and not of others.

Journal Prompt

Do you seek an easy life or expect one of struggle? What absolutes have you created that feed into the limitations you experience?

Empowered Tapping® Script

Use the following script to work through any fears and trauma associated with your past experiences of being rewarded and celebrated to create new possibilities. As you tap each of your meridian points, say this script aloud.

I Am Rewarded and Celebrated

Round 1 (Repeat twice)

TH: Even though it's normal to want to be rewarded and celebrated.

EB: My mind can't just let it be normal.

SE: It has to turn it into an unmet need.

UE: This triggers off my fear responses that I will get stuck in my trauma reactions of feeling punished.

TL: This then sets off a cascade of emotionally painful and traumatic experiences in my mind's reality.

CH: But it's not how my life really has to be.

CB: It's just my fears running stories from my past.

UB: I don't need certain conditions to exist for me to heal from my experiences of not being rewarded and celebrated.

UA: And I don't need specific circumstances to exist for me to transform my fears of feeling punished. I already am accepting being rewarded and celebrated.

Round 2

TH: By interpreting my need to be rewarded and celebrated, being unmet, sets off post-traumatic stress in me I have created a belief that this is how it is and always will be.

EB: That belief that my need to be rewarded and celebrated, being unmet, sets off post-traumatic stress in me is how it is and always will be then colours my experiences, so it feels like it's true.

SE: But it's not true.

UE: By interpreting my need to be rewarded and celebrated, being unmet, sets off post-traumatic stress in me I have created a belief that this is how it is and always will be.

TL: That belief that my need to be rewarded and celebrated, being unmet, sets off post-traumatic stress in me is how it is and always will be then colours my experiences, so it feels like it's true.

CH: But it's not true.

CB: By interpreting my need to be rewarded and celebrated, being unmet, sets off post-traumatic stress in me I have created a belief that this is how it is and always will be.

UB: That belief that my need to be rewarded and celebrated, being unmet, sets off post-traumatic stress in me is how it is and always will be then colours my experiences, so it feels like it's true.

UA: But it's not true.

Round 3

TH: By interpreting my fear of punishment as an expression of post-traumatic stress I have created a belief that this is how it is and always will be.

EB: That belief that my fear of punishment as an expression of post-traumatic stress is how it is and always will be then colours my experiences, so it feels like it's true.

SE: But it's not true.

UE: By interpreting my fear of punishment as an expression of post-traumatic stress I have created a belief that this is how it is and always will be.

TL: That belief that my fear of punishment as an expression of post-traumatic stress is how it is and always will be then colours my experiences, so it feels like it's true.

CH: But it's not true.

CB: By interpreting my fear of punishment as an expression of post-traumatic stress I have created a belief that this is how it is and always will be.

UB: That belief that my fear of punishment as an expression of post-traumatic stress is how it is and always will be then colours my experiences, so it feels like it's true.

UA: But it's not true.

Round 4

All points: I'm letting it all go.

Round 5

TH: The only truth is I already am accepting being rewarded and celebrated.

All remaining points: I already am accepting being rewarded and celebrated.

Cycle 31. Innocence/Blamed

You have the need for innocence, and when this need is not met, you feel blamed. Your fear of being blamed drives you to find ways to re-establish your innocence.

Life is filled with complex interactions around innocence. At points in your life, you will have experiences of feeling blamed by others, and you will create the experience of blaming others. You will perceive blame, even when it is not the intention of others, and you will blame yourself. Your task right now is to identify where this is happening so you can heal the imbalance and align yourself with your true nature.

Through the eyes of innocence, a child sees only love and beauty. They are curious about the delight, adventure and mystery before them. It is a beautiful phase of life. Then, as we grow up, life gets real, more challenging and complex. It can be disappointing to realise that the people you adored and thought were perfect are not. Things may happen that shatter your innocence. Experiencing human nature's darker, more seedy aspects is traumatic and devastating. Complicating things further, you may be blamed for what happens to you, even though you never asked for it. The older you get, the more innocence is lost as you get blamed for more and more things that you may have said or done, even when the outcomes are not as you intended. It may feel as though it doesn't matter if you try to explain your thinking because others are upset and there is no room for understanding or compassion.

Over time, the loss of innocence can translate into you feeling that you are a bad person. It may seem that you are flawed in a way that there is no coming back from. In some instances, you may feel humiliated by who you are. It is so easy to internalise these experiences so that you shame and blame yourself for your true nature. The beliefs you form around the loss of innocence influence your experiences and can draw into you more of the same. This stifles and suffocates you from being your best self.

Self-blame is a coping mechanism designed to help you feel in control. If everything is your fault, then you are responsible for it. That means your words, behaviours and actions can determine the outcome of every event. **Of course, it doesn't always work out as planned because you are only responsible for *your* part.** You aren't responsible for *everything!* As you step back from all this shaming and blaming and embrace the purity of intent, innocence, beauty and your inner child, you will reconnect with the joy, wonder and awe that lives inside you. Yes, your innocence is there, even if it has been tucked away for decades.

Journal Prompt

Take this opportunity to journal about the beauty, joy and wonder that being alive gifts you. Through this, reconnect to your innocence and awe for life's offerings. What are you grateful for?

Empowered Tapping® Script

Use the following script to work through any fears and trauma associated with your past experiences of innocence to create new possibilities. As you tap each of your meridian points, say this script aloud.

I Reignite My Innocence

Round 1 (Repeat twice)

TH: Even though it's normal to want to be innocent.

EB: My mind can't just let it be normal.

SE: It has to turn it into an unmet need.

UE: This triggers off my fear responses that I will get stuck in my trauma reactions of feeling blamed.

TL: This then sets off a cascade of emotionally painful and traumatic experiences in my mind's reality.

CH: But it's not how my life really has to be.

CB: It's just my fears running stories from my past.

UB: I don't need certain conditions to exist for me to heal from my experiences of lost innocence.

UA: And I don't need specific circumstances to exist for me to transform my fears of feeling blamed. I already am reigniting my innocence.

Round 2

TH: By interpreting my need to be innocent, being unmet, sets off post-traumatic stress in me I have created a belief that this is how it is and always will be.

EB: That belief that my need to be innocent, being unmet, sets off post-traumatic stress in me is how it is and always will be then colours my experiences, so it feels like it's true.

SE: But it's not true.

UE: By interpreting my need to be innocent, being unmet, sets off post-traumatic stress in me I have created a belief that this is how it is and always will be.

TL: That belief that my need to be innocent, being unmet, sets off post-traumatic stress in me is how it is and always will be then colours my experiences, so it feels like it's true.

CH: But it's not true.

CB: By interpreting my need to be innocent, being unmet, sets off post-traumatic stress in me I have created a belief that this is how it is and always will be.

UB: That belief that my need to be innocent, being unmet, sets off post-traumatic stress in me is how it is and always will be then colours my experiences, so it feels like it's true.

UA: But it's not true.

Round 3

TH: By interpreting my fear of being blamed as an expression of post-traumatic stress I have created a belief that this is how it is and always will be.

EB: That belief that my fear of being blamed as an expression of post-traumatic stress is how it is and always will be then colours my experiences, so it feels like it's true.

SE: But it's not true.

UE: By interpreting my fear of being blamed as an expression of post-traumatic stress I have created a belief that this is how it is and always will be.

TL: That belief that my fear of being blamed as an expression of post-traumatic stress is how it is and always will be then colours my experiences, so it feels like it's true.

CH: But it's not true.

CB: By interpreting my fear of being blamed as an expression of post-traumatic stress I have created a belief that this is how it is and always will be.

UB: That belief that my fear of being blamed as an expression of post-traumatic stress is how it is and always will be then colours my experiences, so it feels like it's true.

UA: But it's not true.

Round 4

All points: I'm letting it all go.

Round 5

TH: The only truth is I already am reigniting my innocence.

All remaining points: I already am reigniting my innocence.

Cycle 32. Enough/Judged

You have the need to be enough, and when this need is not met, you feel judged. Your fear of being judged drives you to find ways to be enough.

Life is filled with complex interactions around being enough. At points in your life, you will have experiences of feeling judged by others, and you will create the experience of judging others. You will perceive judgement, even when it is not the intention of others, and you will judge yourself. Your task right now is to identify where this is happening so you can heal the imbalance and align yourself with your true nature.

Judgement is associated with something or someone being good or bad. When you feel judged, it's natural to question whether you are good enough, until you accept the universal truth that you are. As you process your life, you will begin by reviewing whether you are 'good enough'. Eventually, you will move beyond that concept and realise that you are unsure whether you are 'enough' just being you. Do you need more of any qualities, traits, behaviours or attitudes? Before you formulate a list, I'm going to jump in and say that we all grow and evolve into ourselves. And right now, in this moment, you are enough. From this place of acceptance, you can become more.

It's important to accept that you are enough from the perspective of love rather than insufficiency or inadequacy. Be aware of any areas where your thoughts align being 'enough' with deserving. If you doubt you are worthy, you will doubt you are enough. Your needs, wants and desires can be thwarted when you cover them with limiting beliefs, such as the idea that you will be deserving of rewards only once you have proven yourself worthy of them. Remember, associating worth with actions destroys its truth. Like worth and existing, being enough just is. Internalising cultural, societal, familial, religious and gendered definitions that place conditions, rules, obligations and duties on your *being* entraps you in the collective acceptance of judgement. True liberation comes as you embrace and live in the knowing that you are enough.

Journal Prompt

Divide a page in your journal into two columns. Title them "The ways I judge myself" and "When I feel judged by others." List how you judge yourself and how you feel judged by others under these headings. Identify the unmet need associated with each judgement.

Empowered Tapping® Script

Create new possibilities by using the following script to work through any fears and trauma associated with your past experiences of being enough. As you tap each of your meridian points, say this script aloud.

I Am Enough

Round 1 (Repeat twice)

TH: Even though it's normal to want to be enough.

EB: My mind can't just let it be normal.

SE: It has to turn it into an unmet need.

UE: This triggers off my fear responses that I will get stuck in my trauma reactions of judgement.

TL: This then sets off a cascade of emotionally painful and traumatic experiences in my mind's reality.

CH: But it's not how my life really has to be.

CB: It's just my fears running stories from my past.

UB: I don't need certain conditions to exist for me to heal from my experiences of not being enough.

UA: And I don't need specific circumstances to exist for me to transform my fears of judgement. I already am enough.

Round 2

TH: By interpreting my need to be enough, being unmet, sets off post-traumatic stress in me I have created a belief that this is how it is and always will be.

EB: That belief that my need to be enough, being unmet, sets off post-traumatic stress in me is how it is and always will be then colours my experiences, so it feels like it's true.

SE: But it's not true.

UE: By interpreting my need to be enough, being unmet, sets off post-traumatic stress in me I have created a belief that this is how it is and always will be.

TL: That belief that my need to be enough, being unmet, sets off post-traumatic stress in me is how it is and always will be then colours my experiences, so it feels like it's true.

CH: But it's not true.

CB: By interpreting my need to be enough, being unmet, sets off post-traumatic stress in me I have created a belief that this is how it is and always will be.

UB: That belief that my need to be enough, being unmet, sets off post-traumatic stress in me is how it is and always will be then colours my experiences, so it feels like it's true.

UA: But it's not true.

Round 3

TH: By interpreting my fear of judgement as an expression of post-traumatic stress I have created a belief that this is how it is and always will be.

EB: That belief that my fear of judgement as an expression of post-traumatic stress is how it is and always will be then colours my experiences, so it feels like it's true.

SE: But it's not true.

UE: By interpreting my fear of judgement as an expression of post-traumatic stress I have created a belief that this is how it is and always will be.

TL: That belief that my fear of judgement as an expression of post-traumatic stress is how it is and always will be then colours my experiences, so it feels like it's true.

CH: But it's not true.

CB: By interpreting my fear of judgement as an expression of post-traumatic stress I have created a belief that this is how it is and always will be.

UB: That belief that my fear of judgement as an expression of post-traumatic stress is how it is and always will be then colours my experiences, so it feels like it's true.

UA: But it's not true.

Round 4

All points: I'm letting it all go.

Round 5

TH: The only truth is I already am enough.

All remaining points: I already am enough.

Cycle 33. Sensual/Undesired

You have the need to feel sensual, and when this need is not met, you feel undesirable. Your fear of being undesired drives you to find ways to feel sensual.

Life is filled with complex interactions around sensuality. At points in your life, you will have experiences of feeling undesired by others, and you will create the experience of undesirability for others. You will perceive being undesired, even when that is not the intention of others, and you will sabotage your sensuality. Your task right now is to identify where this is happening so you can heal the imbalance and align yourself with your true nature.

Your need to be sensual is founded on a want to be wanted, to be attractive and desirable to another and through your own eyes. You want to like who you see in the mirror and to feel good in your body. Sensuality isn't the same as sexuality. Here, sensuality is a respectful desire, unlike lust, which is a sexual desire that's not interested in who you are as a person. Sensuality is joyful sensory engagement, a pleasure that comes from being appreciated and valued by yourself and others. Feeling sensual is an inside job. While people may reject and punish themselves in the hope it will motivate them to change what they don't like about themselves, few respond well to this approach. If it doesn't encourage you to change what you want to change, it's time to let go of your negative inner self-talk. The first step is self-acceptance. It may sound weird, but by accepting where you are, change will eventuate with greater ease. When you care about yourself, you are far more likely to stick to your plan to become the most sensual and desirable version of yourself.

Journal Prompt

Is there something that makes you feel unattractive and, by extension, undesirable? Identify the specifics and then what you can do about it.

Empowered Tapping® Script

Use the following script to work through any fears and trauma associated with your past experiences of sensuality to create new possibilities. As you tap each of your meridian points, say this script aloud.

I Accept My Sensuality

Round 1 (Repeat twice)

TH: Even though it's normal to want to embrace my sensuality.

EB: My mind can't just let it be normal.

SE: It has to turn it into an unmet need.

UE: This triggers off my fear responses that I will get stuck in my trauma reactions of undesirability.

TL: This then sets off a cascade of emotionally painful and traumatic experiences in my mind's reality.

CH: But it's not how my life really has to be.

CB: It's just my fears running stories from my past.

UB: I don't need certain conditions to exist for me to heal from my experiences of sensuality.

UA: And I don't need specific circumstances to exist for me to transform my fears of undesirability. I already am accepting my sensuality.

Round 2

TH: By interpreting my need to be sensual, being unmet, sets off post-traumatic stress in me I have created a belief that this is how it is and always will be.

EB: That belief that my need to be sensual, being unmet, sets off post-traumatic stress in me is how it is and always will be then colours my experiences, so it feels like it's true.

SE: But it's not true.

UE: By interpreting my need to be sensual, being unmet, sets off post-traumatic stress in me I have created a belief that this is how it is and always will be.

TL: That belief that my need to be sensual, being unmet, sets off post-traumatic stress in me is how it is and always will be then colours my experiences, so it feels like it's true.

CH: But it's not true.

CB: By interpreting my need to be sensual, being unmet, sets off post-traumatic stress in me I have created a belief that this is how it is and always will be.

UB: That belief that my need to be sensual, being unmet, sets off post-traumatic stress in me is how it is and always will be then colours my experiences, so it feels like it's true.

UA: But it's not true.

Round 3

TH: By interpreting my fear of undesirability as an expression of post-traumatic stress I have created a belief that this is how it is and always will be.

EB: That belief that my fear of undesirability as an expression of post-traumatic stress is how it is and always will be then colours my experiences, so it feels like it's true.

SE: But it's not true.

UE: By interpreting my fear of undesirability as an expression of post-traumatic stress I have created a belief that this is how it is and always will be.

TL: That belief that my fear of undesirability as an expression of post-traumatic stress is how it is and always will be then colours my experiences, so it feels like it's true.

CH: But it's not true.

CB: By interpreting my fear of undesirability as an expression of post-traumatic stress I have created a belief that this is how it is and always will be.

UB: That belief that my fear of undesirability as an expression of post-traumatic stress is how it is and always will be then colours my experiences, so it feels like it's true.

UA: But it's not true.

Round 4

All points: I'm letting it all go.

Round 5

TH: The only truth is I already am accepting my sensuality.

All remaining points: I already am accepting my sensuality.

Cycle 34. Integrity/Betraying Your Moral Conscience

You have the need to live with integrity, and when this need is not met, you feel guilty of betraying your moral conscience. Your guilt drives you to find ways to live with integrity.

Life is filled with complex interactions around integrity. At points in your life, you will have experiences of feeling like your integrity is being compromised by others, and you will create the experience of compromising integrity for others. You will perceive your integrity as being compromised, even when it is not the intention of others, and you will compromise your own integrity. Your task right now is to identify where this is happening so you can heal the imbalance and align yourself with your true nature.

Every emotion has a purpose, and guilt is no different. You may feel guilty for a number of reasons, and thus, it can have differing purposes. When you betray your morals, ethics, conscience or integrity, guilt can highlight your truth. This type of guilt is a message from your conscience that you are not living according to your personal truth. The guilt serves to motivate you to live in accordance with your values. It may feel challenging to live with integrity in a world that is filled with inconsistency and incongruency. Integrity takes effort and work. It asks you to apply it to your behaviours and actions. According to Stephen L. Carter, professor of law at Yale University, integrity requires three central elements:

1. *Discerning* what is right and wrong.
2. *Acting* on what you have discerned, even at personal cost.
3. *Saying openly* that you are acting on your understanding of right from wrong.

You have undoubtedly encountered people with porous integrity, filled with big words, loud promises and inaction. Our patriarchal society almost encourages this approach to life. But just because society supports certain behaviours, it doesn't mean they are aligned with who you are. Check whether the guilt you feel indicates that you aren't living in your truth. If yes, explore any pressure you feel to compromise yourself from external or inner sources. Accept the struggle to hold onto your truth and live with integrity. Create a plan to overcome this pressure and free yourself from this guilt.

Journal Prompt

What are your moral and ethical guidelines? What creates the circumstances whereby you compromise your conscience?

Empowered Tapping® Script

Use the following script to work through any fears and trauma associated with your past experiences of integrity to create new possibilities. As you tap each of your meridian points, say this script aloud.

I Prioritise My Integrity

Round 1 (Repeat twice)

TH: Even though it's normal to want to live with integrity.

EB: My mind can't just let it be normal.

SE: It has to turn it into an unmet need.

UE: This triggers off my fear responses that I will get stuck in my trauma reactions of betraying my moral conscience.

TL: This then sets off a cascade of emotionally painful and traumatic experiences in my mind's reality.

CH: But it's not how my life really has to be.

CB: It's just my fears running stories from my past.

UB: I don't need certain conditions to exist for me to heal from my experiences of not living with integrity.

UA: And I don't need specific circumstances to exist for me to transform my fears of betraying my moral conscience. I already am prioritising living with integrity.

Round 2

TH: By interpreting my need to live with integrity, being unmet, sets off post-traumatic stress in me I have created a belief that this is how it is and always will be.

EB: That belief that my need to live with integrity, being unmet, sets off post-traumatic stress in me is how it is and always will be then colours my experiences, so it feels like it's true.

SE: But it's not true.

UE: By interpreting my need to live with integrity, being unmet, sets off post-traumatic stress in me l have created a belief that this is how it is and always will be.

TL: That belief that my need to live with integrity, being unmet, sets off post-traumatic stress in me is how it is and always will be then colours my experiences, so it feels like it's true.

CH: But it's not true.

CB: By interpreting my need to live with integrity, being unmet, sets off post-traumatic stress in me l have created a belief that this is how it is and always will be.

UB: That belief that my need to live with integrity, being unmet, sets off post-traumatic stress in me is how it is and always will be then colours my experiences, so it feels like it's true.

UA: But it's not true.

Round 3

TH: By interpreting my fear of betraying my moral conscience as an expression of post-traumatic stress l have created a belief that this is how it is and always will be.

EB: That belief that my fear of betraying my moral conscience as an expression of post-traumatic stress is how it is and always will be then colours my experiences, so it feels like it's true.

SE: But it's not true.

UE: By interpreting my fear of betraying my moral conscience as an expression of post-traumatic stress l have created a belief that this is how it is and always will be.

TL: That belief that my fear of betraying my moral conscience as an expression of post-traumatic stress is how it is and always will be then colours my experiences, so it feels like it's true.

CH: But it's not true.

CB: By interpreting my fear of betraying my moral conscience as an expression of post-traumatic stress l have created a belief that this is how it is and always will be.

UB: That belief that my fear of betraying my moral conscience as an expression of post-traumatic stress is how it is and always will be then colours my experiences, so it feels like it's true.

UA: But it's not true.

Round 4

All points: I'm letting it all go.

Round 5

TH: The only truth is I already am prioritising living with integrity.

All remaining points: I already am prioritising living with integrity.

Cycle 35. Sacred Sexual Connection/Loneliness

You have the need to experience a sacred sexual connection, and when this need is not met, you feel lonely. Your fear of loneliness drives you to find ways to sacredly connect sexually with another.

Life is filled with complex interactions around sacred sexual connection. At points in your life, you will have experiences of feeling lonely, even when with others, and you will create the experience of loneliness for others. You will perceive being lonely, even when it is not the intention of others, and you will feel lonely within yourself. Your task right now is to identify where this is happening so you can heal the imbalance and align yourself with your true nature.

Sacred sexuality asks you to honour the love, beauty and oneness that stems from a deepened connection between yourself and another. It requires a willingness to be vulnerable and discover the strength that lives inside you, knowing that you are whole and complete through the surrender of this union. This state of bliss can sustain you when you are fully aligned with pure love. Where there is a fear of vulnerability, there will be a block to the transcendent nature of sacred connection, and this limits your experience to human sexuality. When fears of rejection, abandonment or unworthiness creep into your actions, you will withhold your true desire and instead seek evidence, proof and validation of your fears. Lack of trust erodes the possibility of forming deep connections. It is easy to stay guarded, alert and suspicious to protect yourself from hurt, but the greatest gift of living in a human body filled with emotions and sensory nerves is sacred connection. A willingness to release your fears and surrender into deeper and deeper experiences of love, connection, joy and happiness through sacred union dissolves any existential loneliness that plagues you. Your soul seeks meaning, unity and purpose through your actions and those you share with others.

Journal Prompt

Describe your sexual relationships in terms of their sacred and connected components.

Empowered Tapping® Script

Use the following script to work through any fears and trauma associated with your past experiences of a sacred sexual connection to create new possibilities. As you tap each of your meridian points, say this script aloud.

I Attract Sacred Sexual Connections

Round 1 (Repeat twice)

TH: Even though it's normal to want to experience sacred sexual connection.

EB: My mind can't just let it be normal.

SE: It has to turn it into an unmet need.

UE: This triggers off my fear responses that I will get stuck in my trauma reactions of loneliness.

TL: This then sets off a cascade of emotionally painful and traumatic experiences in my mind's reality.

CH: But it's not how my life really has to be.

CB: It's just my fears running stories from my past.

UB: I don't need certain conditions to exist for me to heal from my experiences of shallow, pointless sexual interactions.

UA: And I don't need specific circumstances to exist for me to transform my fears of loneliness. I already am attracting a sacred sexual connection.

Round 2

TH: By interpreting my need to experience a sacred sexual connection, being unmet, sets off post-traumatic stress in me I have created a belief that this is how it is and always will be.

EB: That belief that my need to experience a sacred sexual connection, being unmet, sets off post-traumatic stress in me is how it is and always will be then colours my experiences, so it feels like it's true.

SE: But it's not true.

UE: By interpreting my need to experience a sacred sexual connection, being unmet, sets off post-traumatic stress in me I have created a belief that this is how it is and always will be.

TL: That belief that my need to experience a sacred sexual connection, being unmet, sets off post-traumatic stress in me is how it is and always will be then colours my experiences, so it feels like it's true.

CH: But it's not true.

CB: By interpreting my need to experience a sacred sexual connection, being unmet, sets off post-traumatic stress in me I have created a belief that this is how it is and always will be.

UB: That belief that my need to experience a sacred sexual connection, being unmet, sets off post-traumatic stress in me is how it is and always will be then colours my experiences, so it feels like it's true.

UA: But it's not true.

Round 3

TH: By interpreting my fear of loneliness as an expression of post-traumatic stress I have created a belief that this is how it is and always will be.

EB: That belief that my fear of loneliness as an expression of post-traumatic stress is how it is and always will be then colours my experiences, so it feels like it's true.

SE: But it's not true.

UE: By interpreting my fear of loneliness as an expression of post-traumatic stress I have created a belief that this is how it is and always will be.

TL: That belief that my fear of loneliness as an expression of post-traumatic stress is how it is and always will be then colours my experiences, so it feels like it's true.

CH: But it's not true.

CB: By interpreting my fear of loneliness as an expression of post-traumatic stress I have created a belief that this is how it is and always will be.

UB: That belief that my fear of loneliness as an expression of post-traumatic stress is how it is and always will be then colours my experiences, so it feels like it's true.

UA: But it's not true.

Round 4

All points: I'm letting it all go.

Round 5

TH: The only truth is I already am attracting a sacred sexual connection.

All remaining points: I already am attracting a sacred sexual connection.

Cycle 36. Belonging with Like-Minded Souls/The Guilt of Not Belonging

You have the need to belong to a group of like-minded souls, and when this need is not met, you feel guilty. Your guilt for not belonging drives you to find your tribe.

Life is filled with complex interactions around belonging to your tribe. At points in your life, you will have experiences of feeling guilty for not conforming with others, and you will create the experience of guilt for others. You will perceive that you don't belong, even when it is not the intention of others, and you will feel guilty for not being able to do what it takes to belong to family and social groups. Your task right now is to identify where this is happening so you can heal the imbalance and align yourself with your true nature.

In his book, *Acknowledging What Is,* family therapist Bert Hellinger discusses that a sense of belonging to a family helps maintain our innocence, while the fear of not belonging provokes a sense of guilt. In an ideal scenario, family equals common values, ideals and beliefs. Of course, family isn't always a place of shared principles. When they are not, people look outwardly to friends, community and groups to find commonality. Should you perceive that your behaviours, actions, attitudes, feelings and beliefs will lead to rejection, abandonment or no longer belonging, the emotion experienced is guilt. Your fear of not belonging because of who you are creates feelings of guilt. This guilt doesn't help you live a better life. To resolve this guilt, your mind will encourage you to conform to the norms of the group — to give up parts of yourself in order to belong.

When social opportunities are limited, people make friends with those who are available. These friendships are not always based on like-mindedness. In the modern world, where connections can more readily be made with those who have similar interests, people may narrow their friendships to those who share their experiences, perspectives and beliefs. However, this tendency to seek belonging based on familiarity can create challenges. As people change and grow, friendships may fall apart. When the need to belong is met by a group with restrictive membership rules, the fear of rejection and the pressure to conform can create angst and emotional wounding and restrict personal growth.

To resolve the guilt of not belonging, you have to stop looking for validation from the external world. Heal any wounds formed by false cultural, familial, religious and societal beliefs about your worth. When you internalise those beliefs, you create a story in your mind about the conditions and requirements needed to participate in the group you want to belong to. This means you stay focused on making others happy, hoping they will embrace and accept you. Whenever others' behaviours, actions or words aren't what you *need to hear*, you feel guilty, as if you have done something wrong. The challenge with secondary guilt, the guilt of not belonging, is that the process of eliminating it makes you vulnerable to the very fears that feed it in the first place. Like yourself and allow others to form their own opinion of you. It really is possible to communicate, interact and participate in groups without having a desire to be accepted by them. Let go of guilt by letting go of the need to belong to those who refuse to accept you for the person you are.

Journal Prompt

What are your experiences of belonging to a group? How do you feel when you give up parts of yourself to conform?

Empowered Tapping® Script

Create new possibilities by using the following script to work through any fears and trauma associated with your past experiences of belonging to a tribe. As you tap each of your meridian points, say this script aloud.

I Belong with Like-Minded Souls

Round 1 (Repeat twice)

TH: Even though it's normal to want to belong to a group of like-minded souls.

EB: My mind can't just let it be normal.

SE: It has to turn it into an unmet need.

UE: This triggers off my fear responses that I will get stuck in my trauma reactions of feeling guilty.

TL: This then sets off a cascade of emotionally painful and traumatic experiences in my mind's reality.

CH: But it's not how my life really has to be.

CB: It's just my fears running stories from my past.

UB: I don't need certain conditions to exist for me to heal from my experiences of feeling like an outsider.

UA: And I don't need specific circumstances to exist for me to transform my guilt. I already am discovering my tribe.

Round 2

TH: By interpreting my need to belong to a group of like-minded souls, being unmet, sets off post-traumatic stress in me I have created a belief that this is how it is and always will be.

EB: That belief that my need to belong to a group of like-minded souls, being unmet, sets off post-traumatic stress in me is how it is and always will be then colours my experiences, so it feels like it's true.

SE: But it's not true.

UE: By interpreting my need to belong to a group of like-minded souls, being unmet, sets off post-traumatic stress in me I have created a belief that this is how it is and always will be.

TL: That belief that my need to belong to a group of like-minded souls, being unmet, sets off post-traumatic stress in me is how it is and always will be then colours my experiences, so it feels like it's true.

CH: But it's not true.

CB: By interpreting my need to belong to a group of like-minded souls, being unmet, sets off post-traumatic stress in me I have created a belief that this is how it is and always will be.

UB: That belief that my need to belong to a group of like-minded souls, being unmet, sets off post-traumatic stress in me is how it is and always will be then colours my experiences, so it feels like it's true.

UA: But it's not true.

Round 3

TH: By interpreting the guilt I feel if I don't belong as an expression of post-traumatic stress I have created a belief that this is how it is and always will be.

EB: That belief that the guilt I feel if I don't belong as an expression of post-traumatic stress is how it is and always will be then colours my experiences, so it feels like it's true.

SE: But it's not true.

UE: By interpreting the guilt I feel if I don't belong as an expression of post-traumatic stress I have created a belief that this is how it is and always will be.

TL: That belief that the guilt I feel if I don't belong as an expression of post-traumatic stress is how it is and always will be then colours my experiences, so it feels like it's true.

CH: But it's not true.

CB: By interpreting the guilt I feel if I don't belong as an expression of post-traumatic stress I have created a belief that this is how it is and always will be.

UB: That belief that the guilt I feel if I don't belong as an expression of post-traumatic stress is how it is and always will be then colours my experiences, so it feels like it's true.

UA: But it's not true.

Round 4

All points: I'm letting it all go.

Round 5

TH: The only truth is I already am discovering my tribe.

All remaining points: I already am discovering my tribe.

Cycle 37. Purpose/Pointlessness

You have the need to have a sense of purpose, and when this need is not met, you feel lost. Your fear that you are pointless drives you to find ways to justify your presence on earth.

Life is filled with complex interactions around purpose. At points in your life, you will have experiences of feeling pointless to others, and you will create the experience of being pointless for others. You will perceive pointlessness, even when it is not the intention of others, and you will feel pointless within yourself. Your task right now is to identify where this is happening so you can heal the imbalance and align yourself with your true nature.

According to humanistic psychology, we have an internal drive to grow and achieve. In our teenage years, we ask, "Who am I?" By our midlife, we ask, "Why am I here?" The dark night of the soul is a phase where you question everything and experience your own meaninglessness and pointlessness. It's challenging. It's scary. And it's not something anyone wants to embrace. Mostly, people want to run from it. But sitting in your meaninglessness, being completely pointless, and feeling your way through the pain can be the most liberating experience of your life. You will sense your freedom, sovereignty and dignity in a way you have never known. From this void, you are free to re-create yourself without limitations or even expectations. Your liberation from societal, cultural, gendered and familial conditioning opens you to connecting with your purpose, your meaning, the point you want your life to have. You decide. It's not up to anything or anyone else anymore. You choose the priority you give things. You give meaning to your life and the things that happen in it. The point of being lost in the wilderness is to find yourself and live true to your discovery of self with love, presence and knowingness.

Journal Prompt

How would you feel if one of the purposes in your life was to simply be you? What would you have to do to become comfortable enough in your skin to be more of yourself?

Empowered Tapping® Script

Use the following script to work through any fears and trauma associated with your past experiences of purpose to create new possibilities. As you tap each of your meridian points, say this script aloud.

I Am Open To My Purpose

Round 1 (Repeat twice)

TH: Even though it's normal to want a sense of purpose.

EB: My mind can't just let it be normal.

SE: It has to turn it into an unmet need.

UE: This triggers off my fear responses that l will get stuck in my trauma reactions of feeling lost.

TL: This then sets off a cascade of emotionally painful and traumatic experiences in my mind's reality.

CH: But it's not how my life really has to be.

CB: It's just my fears running stories from my past.

UB: I don't need certain conditions to exist for me to heal from my experiences of purposelessness.

UA: And l don't need specific circumstances to exist for me to transform my fears of feeling lost. I already am open to my purpose.

Round 2

TH: By interpreting my need for a sense of purpose, being unmet, sets off post-traumatic stress in me l have created a belief that this is how it is and always will be.

EB: That belief that my need for a sense of purpose, being unmet, sets off post-traumatic stress in me is how it is and always will be then colours my experiences, so it feels like it's true.

SE: But it's not true.

UE: By interpreting my need for a sense of purpose, being unmet, sets off post-traumatic stress in me l have created a belief that this is how it is and always will be.

TL: That belief that my need for a sense of purpose, being unmet, sets off post-traumatic stress in me is how it is and always will be then colours my experiences, so it feels like it's true.

CH: But it's not true.

CB: By interpreting my need for a sense of purpose, being unmet, sets off post-traumatic stress in me I have created a belief that this is how it is and always will be.

UB: That belief that my need for a sense of purpose, being unmet, sets off post-traumatic stress in me is how it is and always will be then colours my experiences, so it feels like it's true.

UA: But it's not true.

Round 3

TH: By interpreting my fear of feeling lost as an expression of post-traumatic stress I have created a belief that this is how it is and always will be.

EB: That belief that my fear of feeling lost as an expression of post-traumatic stress is how it is and always will be then colours my experiences, so it feels like it's true.

SE: But it's not true.

UE: By interpreting my fear of feeling lost as an expression of post-traumatic stress I have created a belief that this is how it is and always will be.

TL: That belief that my fear of feeling lost as an expression of post-traumatic stress is how it is and always will be then colours my experiences, so it feels like it's true.

CH: But it's not true.

CB: By interpreting my fear of feeling lost as an expression of post-traumatic stress I have created a belief that this is how it is and always will be.

UB: That belief that my fear of feeling lost as an expression of post-traumatic stress is how it is and always will be then colours my experiences, so it feels like it's true.

UA: But it's not true.

Round 4

All points: I'm letting it all go.

Round 5

TH: The only truth is I already am open to my purpose.

All remaining points: I already am open to my purpose.

Cycle 38. Whole/Disintegration

You have the need to feel whole, and when this need is not met, you feel like you are falling apart or even losing your mind. Your fear of disintegration drives you to find ways to maintain your wholeness.

Life is filled with complex interactions around being whole. At points in your life, you will have experiences of feeling like you are losing your mind because of others, and you will create the experience of others feeling like they are falling apart. You will perceive crazy-making, even when it is not the intention of others, and you will disintegrate your self-concept through your inner critic. Your task right now is to identify where this is happening so you can heal the imbalance and align yourself with your true nature.

You have many different aspects of your personality. They can come to the fore in the various roles you play in life. Sometimes, they are even opposite and contradictory. You discover who you are through your experiences. Some take you to your limits, while others empower you to shine. The challenge is pulling all the parts of you and your life together in a sense of wholeness. Stressful situations can push you to the point where you feel like you're losing your mind. Others can make you feel like you're crazy for the thoughts you have. There can be phases where you feel like you are falling apart, as if your identity is disintegrating.

Setting boundaries is one of the best skills you can develop in life. You need to know your limits — and you learn them by reaching or passing them. It's important to honour yourself by saying, "That's enough." Once you know your limits, you can integrate all aspects of yourself to create a sense of wholeness.

Journal Prompt

When have you reached your limit in a situation or relationship? Were you able to say when enough was enough? Do you feel capable of setting clear boundaries now?

Empowered Tapping® Script

Use the following script to work through any fears and trauma associated with your past experiences of wholeness to create new possibilities. As you tap each of your meridian points, say this script aloud.

I Integrate My Whole Self

Round 1 (Repeat twice)

TH: Even though it's normal to want to feel whole.

EB: My mind can't just let it be normal.

SE: It has to turn it into an unmet need.

UE: This triggers off my fear responses that I will get stuck in my trauma reactions of falling apart.

TL: This then sets off a cascade of emotionally painful and traumatic experiences in my mind's reality.

CH: But it's not how my life really has to be.

CB: It's just my fears running stories from my past.

UB: I don't need certain conditions to exist for me to heal from my experiences of incompleteness.

UA: And I don't need specific circumstances to exist for me to transform my fears of falling apart. I already am integrating my whole self.

Round 2

TH: By interpreting my need to feel whole, being unmet, sets off post-traumatic stress in me I have created a belief that this is how it is and always will be.

EB: That belief that my need to feel whole, being unmet, sets off post-traumatic stress in me is how it is and always will be then colours my experiences, so it feels like it's true.

SE: But it's not true.

UE: By interpreting my need to feel whole, being unmet, sets off post-traumatic stress in me I have created a belief that this is how it is and always will be.

TL: That belief that my need to feel whole, being unmet, sets off post-traumatic stress in me is how it is and always will be then colours my experiences, so it feels like it's true.

CH: But it's not true.

CB: By interpreting my need to feel whole, being unmet, sets off post-traumatic stress in me I have created a belief that this is how it is and always will be.

UB: That belief that my need to feel whole, being unmet, sets off post-traumatic stress in me is how it is and always will be then colours my experiences, so it feels like it's true.

UA: But it's not true.

Round 3

TH: By interpreting my fear of falling apart as an expression of post-traumatic stress I have created a belief that this is how it is and always will be.

EB: That belief that my fear of falling apart as an expression of post-traumatic stress is how it is and always will be then colours my experiences, so it feels like it's true.

SE: But it's not true.

UE: By interpreting my fear of falling apart as an expression of post-traumatic stress I have created a belief that this is how it is and always will be.

TL: That belief that my fear of falling apart as an expression of post-traumatic stress is how it is and always will be then colours my experiences, so it feels like it's true.

CH: But it's not true.

CB: By interpreting my fear of falling apart as an expression of post-traumatic stress I have created a belief that this is how it is and always will be.

UB: That belief that my fear of falling apart as an expression of post-traumatic stress is how it is and always will be then colours my experiences, so it feels like it's true.

UA: But it's not true.

Round 4

All points: I'm letting it all go.

Round 5

TH: The only truth is I already am integrating my whole self.

All remaining points: I already am integrating my whole self.

Cycle 39. Free and Independent/Trapped

You have the need to be free and independent, and when this need is not met, you feel like you are suffocating under controlling and limiting rules and conditions. Your fear of being trapped drives you to find ways to express your individuality, disentangle yourself from enmeshment and free yourself from imposed ideas of duty and obligation.

Life is filled with complex interactions around freedom and independence. At points in your life, you will have experiences of feeling trapped by others, and you will create the experience of suffocation for others. You will perceive limitations and controls, even when that is not the intention of others, and you will suffocate yourself with your own rules. Your task right now is to identify where this is happening so you can heal the imbalance and align yourself with your true nature.

We humans are funny little creatures. We are social beings wired to bond. Yet, the desire for independence and freedom are aspirations that never leave us. The truth is once we are secure in our connections through love, acceptance, respect and feeling worthy, we are meant to aspire to greater expressions of individuality. As a whole, we are yet to master this. You may find yourself weighing up the desire for freedom and independence. At the very same time, you could be trying to make sense of the voices in your head telling you that you are suffocating under the control of another, that someone's rules and conditions are limiting you from being all you can be. You may resent imposed duty and obligation and be trying to disentangle from enmeshment and co-dependency. Perhaps you feel trapped or that you are asking for help, but no one can hear you. However, like a bird trapped in their cage with the door open, there may be some comfort in blaming the cage for your lack of freedom.

You already are an individual. You can choose what you do and how you do it. You may feel guilty when you don't meet the expectations of others, but that's just an emotion. Emotions can be healed, transformed and resolved. You are free. You are independent. The rest is just external noise that you can manage. You can navigate the social, cultural, gendered, generational and familial rules to be true to yourself. You can also do it respectfully without severing relationships.

Journal Prompt

What cultural cage creates your perceived or actual limitations? What is it about being free and independent that scares you?

Empowered Tapping® Script

Use the following script to work through any fears and trauma associated with your past experiences of being free and independent to create new possibilities. As you tap each of your meridian points, say this script aloud.

I Am Free To Express My Independent Self

Round 1 (Repeat twice)

TH: Even though it's normal to want to be free and independent.

EB: My mind can't just let it be normal.

SE: It has to turn it into an unmet need.

UE: This triggers off my fear responses that I will get stuck in my trauma reactions of entrapment.

TL: This then sets off a cascade of emotionally painful and traumatic experiences in my mind's reality.

CH: But it's not how my life really has to be.

CB: It's just my fears running stories from my past.

UB: I don't need certain conditions to exist for me to heal from my experiences of suffocation under the control of another.

UA: And I don't need specific circumstances to exist for me to transform my fears of entrapment. I already am finding ways to express my individuality.

Round 2

TH: By interpreting my need to be free and independent, being unmet, sets off post-traumatic stress in me I have created a belief that this is how it is and always will be.

EB: That belief that my need to be free and independent, being unmet, sets off post-traumatic stress in me is how it is and always will be then colours my experiences, so it feels like it's true.

SE: But it's not true.

UE: By interpreting my need to be free and independent, being unmet, sets off post-traumatic stress in me I have created a belief that this is how it is and always will be.

TL: That belief that my need to be free and independent, being unmet, sets off post-traumatic stress in me is how it is and always will be then colours my experiences, so it feels like it's true.

CH: But it's not true.

CB: By interpreting my need to be free and independent, being unmet, sets off post-traumatic stress in me I have created a belief that this is how it is and always will be.

UB: That belief that my need to be free and independent, being unmet, sets off post-traumatic stress in me is how it is and always will be then colours my experiences, so it feels like it's true.

UA: But it's not true.

Round 3

TH: By interpreting my fear of entrapment as an expression of post-traumatic stress I have created a belief that this is how it is and always will be.

EB: That belief that my fear of entrapment as an expression of post-traumatic stress is how it is and always will be then colours my experiences, so it feels like it's true.

SE: But it's not true.

UE: By interpreting my fear of entrapment as an expression of post-traumatic stress I have created a belief that this is how it is and always will be.

TL: That belief that my fear of entrapment as an expression of post-traumatic stress is how it is and always will be then colours my experiences, so it feels like it's true.

CH: But it's not true.

CB: By interpreting my fear of entrapment as an expression of post-traumatic stress I have created a belief that this is how it is and always will be.

UB: That belief that my fear of entrapment as an expression of post-traumatic stress is how it is and always will be then colours my experiences, so it feels like it's true.

UA: But it's not true.

Round 4

All points: I'm letting it all go.

Round 5

TH: The only truth is I already am finding ways to express my individuality.

All remaining points: I already am finding ways to express my individuality.

Cycle 40. Shining Brightly/Dulled

You have the need to shine brightly, and when this need is not met, you feel dulled. Your fear of being dulled drives you to find ways to shine brightly.

Life is filled with complex interactions around shining brightly. At points in your life, you will have experiences of feeling dulled by others, and you will create the experience of dulling others. You will perceive being dulled, even when it is not the intention of others, and you will dull your own shine. Your task right now is to identify where this is happening so you can heal the imbalance and align yourself with your true nature.

Many cultures have an attitude that dulls others' shine. In Australia and New Zealand, we refer to cutting down those who rise too high as 'Tall Poppy Syndrome'. Our egalitarian principles of a fair go for all may be offered as justification. But it's not a fair go. It is an intentional act to dull those who are gifted or talented or just fully embracing their purpose. Other countries have their own sayings. In Japan, they say, "The nail that sticks up gets hammered down." And in the Netherlands, "Don't put your head above ground level." Scandinavia has the Law of Jante, which says, "You're not to think you are anything special" and "Perhaps you don't think *we* know a few things about *you*?"

Yet, the drive to shine brightly and be the very best you can be is continually calling you. A great inner stress is felt as the desire to be more is confronted with examples of how society loves to cut those who shine down to size. If the media can't find something shameful to discredit them with, they will just make it up. It's enough to make you want to crawl under your rock and stay there ... and that's exactly what it is intended to do. Sometimes, being dulled and numb feels safer than stepping outside your comfort zone. Hiding behind excess kilos, busying yourself doing a lot or not much at all, using all your energy processing childhood trauma or becoming lost in drama are highly effective methods to stay dull and avoid shining brightly. You can spend your whole life consumed in this version of your life story. Or, you can write a new chapter filled with challenges, adventures, mistakes, failures, learning, laughter and delight. Connect to the joy of living as your best self and shine brightly for all to see.

Journal Prompt

What is stopping you from shining brightly?

Empowered Tapping® Script

Use the following script to work through any fears and trauma associated with your past experiences of shining brightly to create new possibilities. As you tap each of your meridian points, say this script aloud.

I Shine Brightly

Round 1 (Repeat twice)

TH: Even though it's normal to want to shine brightly.

EB: My mind can't just let it be normal.

SE: It has to turn it into an unmet need.

UE: This triggers off my fear responses that I will get stuck in my trauma reactions of dullness.

TL: This then sets off a cascade of emotionally painful and traumatic experiences in my mind's reality.

CH: But it's not how my life really has to be.

CB: It's just my fears running stories from my past.

UB: I don't need certain conditions to exist for me to heal from my experiences of not being allowed to shine brightly.

UA: And I don't need specific circumstances to exist for me to transform my fears of being dulled. I already am accepting opportunities to shine brightly.

Round 2

TH: By interpreting my need to shine brightly, being unmet, sets off post-traumatic stress in me I have created a belief that this is how it is and always will be.

EB: That belief that my need to shine brightly, being unmet, sets off post-traumatic stress in me is how it is and always will be then colours my experiences, so it feels like it's true.

SE: But it's not true.

UE: By interpreting my need to shine brightly, being unmet, sets off post-traumatic stress in me I have created a belief that this is how it is and always will be.

TL: That belief that my need to shine brightly, being unmet, sets off post-traumatic stress in me is how it is and always will be then colours my experiences, so it feels like it's true.

CH: But it's not true.

CB: By interpreting my need to shine brightly, being unmet, sets off post-traumatic stress in me I have created a belief that this is how it is and always will be.

UB: That belief that my need to shine brightly, being unmet, sets off post-traumatic stress in me is how it is and always will be then colours my experiences, so it feels like it's true.

UA: But it's not true.

Round 3

TH: By interpreting my fear of being dulled as an expression of post-traumatic stress I have created a belief that this is how it is and always will be.

EB: That belief that my fear of being dulled as an expression of post-traumatic stress is how it is and always will be then colours my experiences, so it feels like it's true.

SE: But it's not true.

UE: By interpreting my fear of being dulled as an expression of post-traumatic stress I have created a belief that this is how it is and always will be.

TL: That belief that my fear of being dulled as an expression of post-traumatic stress is how it is and always will be then colours my experiences, so it feels like it's true.

CH: But it's not true.

CB: By interpreting my fear of being dulled as an expression of post-traumatic stress I have created a belief that this is how it is and always will be.

UB: That belief that my fear of being dulled as an expression of post-traumatic stress is how it is and always will be then colours my experiences, so it feels like it's true.

UA: But it's not true.

Round 4

All points: I'm letting it all go.

Round 5

TH: The only truth is I already am accepting opportunities to shine brightly.

All remaining points: I already am accepting opportunities to shine brightly.

Empowered Realisms

This section includes the seven Empowered Realism philosophies, each accompanied by journal prompts to help you understand their implications in your life.

The Empowered Tapping® scripts provided here are designed to peel away layers of limiting beliefs, guiding you towards greater self-awareness and transformation.

Empowered Realism 1. Your Beliefs Are Always Right

Beliefs are always proven true. As the saying goes, "Whether you believe you can or believe you can't, you are right." You create circumstances that validate your beliefs and interpret your experiences through your beliefs. Both scenarios ensure your beliefs perpetuate themselves. As your beliefs inform your perceptions, they colour how you interpret your reality. Everything you think is a belief. Whatever you say stems from the idea that you believe it — and from your perspective and experience it is true. Some beliefs formed by your experiences build on and support the best in you while others create a perception of struggle, isolation and limitation. No matter what beliefs you form, they are where your focus will be and what you will bring into your life.

Journal Prompt

When have you created circumstances that validate your beliefs? When have you interpreted your experiences in a way that perpetuates your patterns?

Empowered Tapping® Script

Use the following script to work through the limitations created by the idea that your beliefs are always right to create new possibilities. As you tap each of your meridian points, say this script aloud.

My Beliefs Are My Experience

Round 1 (Repeat twice)

TH: Even though it's normal to always prove my beliefs right.

EB: It's not always helpful.

SE: My mind plays tricks on me so I never see the link between what I think and what I experience.

UE: This triggers off my fear responses that I will keep creating the circumstances that will validate my beliefs.

TL: This then sets off a cascade of emotionally painful experiences in my mind's reality.

CH: But it's not how my life really has to be.

CB: It's just my fears running stories from my past.

UB: I don't really need certain conditions to exist for me to recognise the link between my thoughts and what I experience.

UA: And I don't need specific circumstances to exist for me to recognise the link between my thoughts and what I experience. I already am recognising the link between my thoughts and what I experience.

Round 2

TH: By interpreting I never see the link between what I think and what I experience as being about me I have created a belief that this is how it is and always will be.

EB: That belief that I never see the link between what I think and what I experience is how it is and always will be then colours my experiences, so it feels like it's true.

SE: But it's not true.

UE: By interpreting I never see the link between what I think and what I experience as being about me I have created a belief that this is how it is and always will be.

TL: That belief that I never see the link between what I think and what I experience is how it is and always will be then colours my experiences, so it feels like it's true.

CH: But it's not true.

CB: By interpreting I never see the link between what I think and what I experience as being about me I have created a belief that this is how it is and always will be.

UB: That belief that I never see the link between what I think and what I experience is how it is and always will be then colours my experiences, so it feels like it's true.

UA: But it's not true.

Round 3

TH: By interpreting my experiences through my beliefs I ensure I perpetuate them as being about me I have created a belief that this is how it is and always will be.

EB: That belief that I interpret my experiences through my beliefs ensuring I perpetuate them is how it is and always will be then colours my experiences, so it feels like it's true.

SE: But it's not true.

UE: By interpreting my experiences through my beliefs I ensure I perpetuate them as being about me I have created a belief that this is how it is and always will be.

TL: That belief that I interpret my experiences through my beliefs ensuring I perpetuate them is how it is and always will be then colours my experiences, so it feels like it's true.

CH: But it's not true.

CB: By interpreting my experiences through my beliefs I ensure I perpetuate them as being about me I have created a belief that this is how it is and always will be.

UB: That belief that I interpret my experiences through my beliefs ensuring I perpetuate them is how it is and always will be then colours my experiences, so it feels like it's true.

UA: But it's not true.

Round 4

All points: I'm letting it all go.

Round 5

TH: The only truth is I already am recognising the link between my thoughts and what I experience.

All remaining points: I already am recognising the link between my thoughts and what I experience.

Empowered Realism 2. To Every Rule An Exception

We all create rules to give structure to our lives. You are no exception. Since you were a small child, you have interpreted your experiences and absorbed the conditioning you have been exposed to from family, media, society, religion and your culture to create a sense of security and stability. Within themselves, rules are not wrong or bad, but when you make rules mean more than they need to, life gets more complicated. Having boundaries, guidelines, limitations and defining lines as to what is acceptable and unacceptable, tolerable and intolerable, not enough and too much helps you manoeuvre through life. The complication is that to every rule there is an exception. While a rule may work in a particular situation or for a certain kind of person, it won't work in all scenarios or for all people. There are exceptions. Stress is created when you say, "But this is the rule; it's meant to be this way." When the world or other people don't act according to your rules, you can end up all bent out of shape because things and people *should* be a certain way. When you get hung up on the *shoulds, oughts, musts* and *meant-to-be's,* rules become unhelpful and unproductive.

Journal Prompt

How do you respond when life doesn't reflect your ideas about how things should be? List the *shoulds, oughts, musts* and *meant-to-be's* you hear running through your mind for a week. Write about what you discover.

Empowered Tapping® Script

Use the following script to embrace the idea that every rule you create has exceptions that open you to new possibilities. As you tap each of your meridian points, say this script aloud.

Every Rule Has Exceptions

Round 1 (Repeat twice)

TH: Even though it's normal for me to create rules to give my life structure and security.

EB: My mind can't just let them stay as guidelines.

SE: It tends to turn them into rigid and inflexible obligations.

UE: This triggers off my fear responses that to every rule I make there is an exception.

TL: This then sets off a cascade of emotionally painful experiences in my mind's reality.

CH: But it's not how my life really has to be.

CB: It's just my fears running stories from my past.

UB: I don't really need certain conditions to exist for me to be flexible in dealing with life as it comes.

UA: And I don't need specific circumstances to exist for me to remain flexible in dealing with life as it comes. I already am flexible in dealing with life as it comes.

Round 2

TH: By interpreting I make rules mean more than they have to as being about me I have created a belief that it stresses me if to every rule I make there is an exception.

EB: That belief that it stresses me if to every rule I make there is an exception then colours my experiences, so it feels like it's all that is possible.

SE: But it's not all that is possible.

UE: By interpreting I make rules mean more than they have to as being about me I have created a belief that it stresses me if to every rule I make there is an exception.

TL: That belief that it stresses me if to every rule I make there is an exception then colours my experiences, so it feels like it's all that is possible.

CH: But it's not all that is possible.

CB: By interpreting I make rules mean more than they have to as being about me I have created a belief that it stresses me if to every rule I make there is an exception.

UB: That belief that it stresses me if to every rule I make there is an exception then colours my experiences, so it feels like it's all that is possible.

UA: But it's not all that is possible.

Round 3

All points: I'm letting it all go.

Round 4

TH: The only truth is I already am flexible in dealing with life as it comes.

All remaining points: I already am flexible in dealing with life as it comes.

Empowered Realism 3. Sometimes It's About You, Sometimes It's Not

Too often, the self-help industry tells you that everything is about you – that everyone and everything are reflections of an aspect of yourself. Well, guess what? Sometimes it is about you and sometimes it's not. Either way, there can always be lessons to learn but that doesn't mean taking responsibility for the whole situation will improve things. A good dose of reality comes in handy about now. You aren't in control and, therefore, are not responsible for what anyone (who is not your child under the age of 12) does, thinks, feels or acts out. You are, however, responsible for your part in any situation. That is what is about you. What is not about you is the part that someone else is responsible for. The tricky bit is that too often, you try to make things about yourself that are really about others — and then abdicate your responsibility for your part. Or you claim you are responsible for what someone else said or did because you have merged with this other person, don't want to hold them accountable or feel guilty by association — *if they did it, it's my fault*. The cycle of misplaced responsibility, shame and blame will continue while you take responsibility for things that are not of your doing and don't take responsibility for your words, behaviours and actions.

Journal Prompt

Where have you tried to make things about yourself because you were trying to manage a situation, so it was less stressful for you? When have you abdicated your responsibility and blamed another for your part in a situation?

Empowered Tapping® Script

Use the following script to work through the confusion created by the duality of things being about you and not being about you to create new possibilities. As you tap each of your meridian points, say this script aloud.

Sometimes It's Me, Sometimes It's Not

Round 1 (Repeat twice)

TH: Even though it's normal for me to get confused about what is about me and what isn't.

EB: It's not normal.

SE: It's just the conditioning I have absorbed that traps me in confusion.

UE: This triggers off my fear responses that this is how it is and always will be.

TL: This then sets off a cascade of emotionally painful experiences in my mind's reality.

CH: But it's not how my life really has to be.

CB: It's just my fears running stories from my past.

UB: I don't really need certain conditions to exist for me to discern what is my responsibility.

UA: And I don't need specific circumstances to exist for me to discern what is someone else's responsibility. I already am clearly discerning between what is my responsibility and what is someone else's.

Round 2

TH: By interpreting I get confused about what is about me and what is about someone else as being about me I have experienced a reality where this is how it is and always will be.

EB: This reality where I get confused about what is about me and what is about someone else is how it is and always will be then colours my experiences so it feels like it's true.

SE: But it's not true.

UE: By interpreting I get confused about what is about me and what is about someone else as being about me I have experienced a reality where this is how it is and always will be.

TL: This reality where I get confused about what is about me and what is about someone else is how it is and always will be then colours my experiences so it feels like it's true.

CH: But it's not true.

CB: By interpreting I get confused about what is about me and what is about someone else as being about me I have experienced a reality where this is how it is and always will be.

UB: This reality where I get confused about what is about me and what is about someone else is how it is and always will be then colours my experiences so it feels like it's true.

UA: But it's not true.

Round 3

All points: I am letting it all go.

Round 4

TH: The only truth is I already am clearly discerning between what is my responsibility and what is someone else's.

All remaining points: I already am clearly discerning between what is my responsibility and what is someone else's.

Empowered Realism 4. BIG-You and Small-You

The BIG-you is all-knowing, aware and observes the events and interactions in your life for what they are. This part of you can see and understand your personal story — your big picture, the grander picture, the spiritual journey and the purpose or reason you came here. It is the calm observer who isn't flustered by immediate circumstances but holds an optimistic perspective that things will always work out and are as they are meant to be at any given moment.

The small-you believes everything you experience is real and all there is. It feels the hurts and pains of life deeply, including your childhood memories. It lives in the world, taking on the beliefs of parents, family, friends and society. It interprets your experiences through the external perceptions provided by the outer world. It is fear-based. The small-you is run by the amygdala and is always trying to keep you safe from danger, even if that danger is being the best you can be!

The BIG-you and the small-you make up the mental chatter in your head. The negative voice is the small-you and is often labelled the 'inner critic'. The positive voice, your inner best friend is the BIG-you. When the BIG-you supports and nurtures the small-you, you parent yourself to a fuller, more enjoyable life.

Journal Prompt

Observe your thoughts and record the times when the BIG-you speaks loudest and when the small-you dominates your interpretations.

Empowered Tapping® Script

Use the following script to work through your experiences of your BIG-you and small-you to create new possibilities. As you tap each of your meridian points, say this script aloud.

Big Me, Small Me

Round 1 (Repeat twice)

TH: Even though it's normal to want to put my experiences into context.

EB: My mind just can't let it be normal.

SE: It has to turn it into an unmet need.

UE: This triggers off my fear responses that I'm stuck in experiencing the patterns that happen in my life.

TL: This then sets off a cascade of emotionally painful experiences in my mind's reality.

CH: But it's not how my life really has to be.

CB: It's just my fears running stories from my past.

UB: I don't really need certain conditions to exist for me to comprehend the bigger picture occurring now.

UA: And I don't need specific circumstances to exist for me to comprehend the bigger picture playing out now. I already am comprehending the bigger picture of my life.

Round 2

TH: By interpreting life through the eyes of my small self as being about me I have created a reality where I'm stuck in experiencing the patterns that happen in my life.

EB: This reality where I'm stuck in experiencing the patterns that happen in my life then colours my experiences so it feels like all I can do.

SE: But it's not all I can do.

UE: By interpreting life through the eyes of my small-self as being about me I have created a reality where I'm stuck in experiencing the patterns that happen in my life.

TL: This reality where I'm stuck in experiencing the patterns that happen in my life then colours my experiences so it feels like all I can do.

CH: But it's not all I can do.

CB: By interpreting life through the eyes of my small-self as being about me I have created a reality where I'm stuck in experiencing the patterns that happen in my life.

UB: This reality where I'm stuck in experiencing the patterns that happen in my life then colours my experiences so it feels like all I can do.

UA: But it's not all I can do.

Round 3

All points: I'm letting it all go.

Round 4

TH: The only truth is I already am comprehending the bigger picture of my life.

All remaining points: I already am comprehending the bigger picture of my life.

Empowered Realism 5. It's All Just Data: Information You Can Utilise

The information you take in via your sensory organs—eyes, ears, nose, taste buds, skin—arrives in your limbic system. The organs that interpret this data include the amygdala, hippocampus, reticular activating system and thalamus. The conversations between these parts of your limbic system happen within nanoseconds. They aim to help you respond to your current situation by pulling memories from similar experiences in your past. That information is overlaid with your sense of self-worth and self-esteem and mixed with your needs and fears to generate a thick and textured reaction. Learning to create space between an event and your reaction gives you time to reply to the limbic response. An amazing thing happens when you think of that response as being nothing more than data. Your brain says, "Oh! Okay, well, in that case, isn't that interesting." You then get to choose your response and once in charge of your mind, you are no longer controlled by your emotional reactions. With this shift, the drama and personalisation that have defined your life begin to dissolve.

Journal Prompt

Consider your emotional and physical response to a past or present situation. How does your brain respond when you view its interpretation as data you could utilise?

Empowered Tapping® Script

Use the following script to work through your experience of how your limbic system turns everything into a drama. Create new possibilities as you tap each of your meridian points while saying this script aloud.

It's Just Data

Round 1 (Repeat twice)

TH: Even though it's normal for my brain to turn data into drama.

EB: It's not very helpful.

SE: It's just how the amygdala communicates with the other parts of the limbic system.

UE: This triggers off my fear responses that I will always be stuck in drama and personalising interactions.

TL: This then sets off a cascade of emotionally painful experiences in my mind's reality.

CH: But it's not how my life really has to be.

CB: It's just my fears running stories from my past.

UB: I don't really need certain conditions to exist for me to de-dramatize my interpretations.

UA: And I don't need specific circumstances to exist for me to de-personalise my interactions. I already am accepting that it's all just data I can utilise to make sense of my life.

Round 2

TH: By interpreting I am stuck in drama as being about me I have created a belief that this is how it is and always will be.

EB: That belief that I am stuck in drama is how it is and always will be then colours my experiences, so it feels like it's true.

SE: But it's not true.

UE: By interpreting I am stuck in drama as being about me I have created a belief that this is how it is and always will be.

TL: That belief that I am stuck in drama is how it is and always will be then colours my experiences, so it feels like it's true.

CH: But it's not true.

CB: By interpreting I am stuck in drama as being about me I have created a belief that this is how it is and always will be.

UB: That belief that I am stuck in drama is how it is and always will be then colours my experiences, so it feels like it's true.

UA: But it's not true.

Round 3

TH: By interpreting I am stuck in personalising interactions as being about me I have created a belief that this is how it is and always will be.

EB: That belief that I am stuck in personalising interactions is how it is and always will be then colours my experiences, so it feels like it's true.

SE: But it's not true.

UE: By interpreting I am stuck in personalising interactions as being about me I have created a belief that this is how it is and always will be.

TL: That belief that I am stuck in personalising interactions is how it is and always will be then colours my experiences, so it feels like it's true.

CH: But it's not true.

CB: By interpreting I am stuck in personalising interactions as being about me I have created a belief that this is how it is and always will be.

UB: That belief that I am stuck in personalising interactions is how it is and always will be then colours my experiences, so it feels like it's true.

UA: But it's not true.

Round 4

All points: I'm letting it all go.

Round 5

TH: The only truth is I already am accepting that it's all just data I can utilise to make sense of my life.

All remaining points: I already am accepting that it's all just data I can utilise to make sense of my life.

Empowered Realism 6. Proportional Response

The principle of proportional response suggests that the intensity of behaviours, words and actions reflects how strongly an emotion is felt. In other words, the degree to which you feel something is mirrored in your behaviours, words and actions. Likewise, the degree to which someone else feels something is reflected in their behaviours, words and actions. The stronger the feelings, the more extreme the behaviours, the harsher the words and the more irrational the actions. Too often, we judge the seemingly bizarre outbursts of others as them losing their minds. We also judge ourselves when we hysterically blurt out our deepest fears or wounds. As a society, we don't do well at holding space for people's responses, especially when they seem disproportionate to the circumstances. As we don't know what is happening in another's life, the general advice is to respond to people with kindness. It's a great idea, but it doesn't always happen in the moment. Still, I'm going to pitch it to you. Whether responding to yourself or someone else, try to stop the internal drama or the external personalisation just long enough to ask yourself, "What unmet need is triggering this intense response?"

Journal Prompt

Consider a time when your actions seemed to be disproportionate to the situation. What unmet needs can you identify as the triggers of your behaviour, words or actions?

Empowered Tapping® Script

Use the following script to work through your responses to experiences to create new possibilities. As you tap each of your meridian points, say this script aloud.

Proportional Response

Round 1 (Repeat twice)

TH: Even though it's normal for me to respond proportionately to the degree my needs are not being met.

EB: It's not normal.

SE: It's just my amygdala demanding things be on its terms.

UE: This triggers off my fear responses that this is how it is and always will be.

TL: This then sets off a cascade of emotionally painful experiences in my mind's reality.

CH: But it's not how my life really has to be.

CB: It's just my fears running stories from my past.

UB: I don't really need certain conditions to exist for me to slow my amygdala's responses down.

UA: And I don't need specific circumstances to exist for me to direct my thoughts into life-affirming perspectives. I already am responding proportionally to my experiences.

Round 2

TH: By interpreting my amygdala's demand things be on its terms as being about me I have created a belief that this is how it is and always will be.

EB: That belief that my amygdala demands things be on its terms is how it is and always will be then colours my experiences, so it feels like it's true.

SE: But it's not true.

UE: By interpreting my amygdala's demand things be on its terms as being about me I have created a belief that this is how it is and always will be.

TL: That belief that my amygdala demands things be on its terms is how it is and always will be then colours my experiences, so it feels like it's true.

CH: But it's not true.

CB: By interpreting my amygdala's demand things be on its terms as being about me I have created a belief that this is how it is and always will be.

UB: That belief that my amygdala demands things be on its terms is how it is and always will be then colours my experiences, so it feels like it's true.

UA: But it's not true.

Round 3

TH: By interpreting the intensity of my reactions to not having my needs met as a being about me I have created a belief that this is how it is and always will be.

EB: That belief that the intensity of my reactions to not having my needs met is how it is and always will be then colours my experiences, so it feels like it's true.

SE: But it's not true.

UE: By interpreting the intensity of my reactions to not having my needs met as a being about me l have created a belief that this is how it is and always will be.

TL: That belief that the intensity of my reactions to not having my needs met is how it is and always will be then colours my experiences, so it feels like it's true.

CH: But it's not true.

CB: By interpreting the intensity of my reactions to not having my needs met as a being about me l have created a belief that this is how it is and always will be.

UB: That belief that the intensity of my reactions to not having my needs met is how it is and always will be then colours my experiences, so it feels like it's true.

UA: But it's not true.

Round 4

All points: I'm letting it all go.

Round 5

TH: The only truth is I already am responding proportionally to my experiences.

All remaining points: I already am responding proportionally to my experiences.

Empowered Realism 7. Your Experiences Don't Make You Who You Are

Your life experiences don't always make you who you are, despite it being a popular axiom. There is a *you* that has always existed. The real you won't disappear due to dysfunctional, less-than-nurturing experiences. As you venture on your healing journey, you erroneously equate the experience with the 'making of who you are' instead of recognising that who you are has always existed. Once you peel away the false beliefs, there is only you. Additionally, people may say you are a nice person *because* of your experiences. The truth is that you remained nice *despite* all you have experienced. You could have turned mean and nasty, but it wasn't in your nature. And that nature existed before your experiences — positive and negative. Those who become nasty or negative, supposedly due to their experiences, already have those qualities within their nature. There is a caution to be had in this adage as well. When you believe the only way to grow as a person is to go through hardship, you create the circumstances for suffering so that you can learn to be kinder or wiser. That doesn't make a lot of sense.

Journal Prompt

Write the story of your life. Write about how you responded during the significant events of your life. Describe who you have always been.

Empowered Tapping® Script

Use the following script to work through the limitations created by the idea that your experiences make you who you are. Create new possibilities as you tap each of your meridian points while saying this script aloud.

I Am Not My Experiences

Round 1 (Repeat twice)

TH: Even though it's normal for me to think my experiences make me who I am.

EB: It's not normal.

SE: It's just the rules about how to heal that give credit to the negative experiences in my life.

UE: This triggers off my fear responses that I can only be a better person through suffering.

TL: This then sets off a cascade of emotionally painful experiences in my mind's reality.

CH: But it's not how my life really has to be.

CB: It's just my fears running stories from my past.

UB: I don't really need certain conditions to exist for me to connect with whom I have always been.

UA: And I don't need specific circumstances to exist for me to connect with whom I have always been. I already am connecting to whom I have always been.

Round 2

TH: By interpreting my experiences make me who I am as being about me I have created a belief that I can only be a better person through suffering.

EB: That belief that I can only be a better person through suffering then colours my experiences, so it feels like it's true.

SE: But it's not true.

UE: By interpreting my experiences make me who I am as being about me I have created a belief that I can only be a better person through suffering.

TL: That belief that I can only be a better person through suffering then colours my experiences, so it feels like it's true.

CH: But it's not true.

CB: By interpreting my experiences make me who I am as being about me I have created a belief that I can only be a better person through suffering.

UB: That belief that I can only be a better person through suffering then colours my experiences, so it feels like it's true.

UA: But it's not true.

Round 3

TH: By interpreting my experiences make me who I am as being about me I have created a belief that this is how it is and always will be.

EB: That belief that my experiences make me who I am is how it is and always will be then colours my experiences, so it feels like it's true.

SE: But it's not true.

UE: By interpreting my experiences make me who I am as being about me I have created a belief that this is how it is and always will be.

TL: That belief that my experiences make me who I am is how it is and always will be then colours my experiences, so it feels like it's true.

CH: But it's not true.

CB: By interpreting my experiences make me who I am as being about me I have created a belief that this is how it is and always will be.

UB: That belief that my experiences make me who I am is how it is and always will be then colours my experiences, so it feels like it's true.

UA: But it's not true.

Round 4

All points: I'm letting it all go.

Round 5

TH: The only truth is I already am connecting to whom I have always been.

All remaining points: I already am connecting to whom I have always been.

Emotional Continuums

In the intricate landscape of human emotions, your internal world is a tapestry interwoven with threads of unmet needs and connected fears. As you navigate the complexities of your feelings, it becomes evident that the expression of 'small-t's' (small traumas) is a process distinct from your immediate emotional responses. This realisation marks the beginning of your journey into the realm of emotional continuums, a chapter where we delve into the nuanced spectrum of your emotional experiences.

Emotions, regarded as your internal guidance system, manifest in various forms — anger, anxiety, depression, guilt, jealousy and shame, to name a few. The challenge lies in our collective inability to effectively manage and comprehend this rich tapestry of feelings. The time has come to understand emotions not as isolated entities but as interconnected family groups to pave the way for a more refined self-awareness. As a tool, the purpose of the emotional continuums is to identify and articulate your emotions beyond the familiar surface zone. In this section, we unravel ten continuums: anger, fear, shame, jealousy, guilt, grief, depression, trauma, powerlessness and sabotage. These emotions range from softer expressions to more intense manifestations within each category.

You may have uttered or heard phrases like, "I'm not angry; I'm frustrated." Being able to distinguish between emotions like this is beneficial. Frustration represents a softer facet of anger. The continuums, therefore, serve as a linguistic guide, helping you accurately name and understand the depth of your emotions. They offer a vocabulary for your feelings and a lens through which you can recognise habitual emotional patterns.

In a society that historically shaped gender roles and expectations, boys were often encouraged to suppress tears and embrace anger, while girls were steered to express anger through tears. These societal norms can replace authentic emotional expression with conditioned responses. I invite you to challenge these conditioned responses while encouraging the expression of the appropriate emotion for each unique experience. Whether it is acknowledging sadness instead of defaulting to anger or embracing anger without the veil of tears, the goal is authentic emotional expression.

Emotional continuums not only empower you to name your true feelings but also serve as a compass for navigating life's emotional terrain. By unravelling the threads of conditioned response, you reconnect with your internal guidance system and foster more authentic and calm emotional expression. Venture further into self-discovery as we search for the transformative potential within the spectrum of emotional continuums and insert the emotions into the Empowered Tapping® for Emotional Continuums Template.

The Anger Continuum

Annoyance — frustration — discontent — impatience — sulkiness —crankiness — irritability — petulance — upset — offence — indignation — insult — anger — rile — bitterness — resentment — disgust — repulsion — loathing — hostility — hatred — rage.

The Fear Continuum

Shyness — unease — nervousness — timidness — apprehension — wariness — concern — inactivity — fearfulness — anxiousness — worry — scared — afraid — hypersensitivity — overcautious — uncomfortable — vulnerability — frightened — hysteria — catastrophising — dread — shock — frenzy — panic — resistance — repressed feelings — suppressed feelings — terrified — petrified — horrified.

The Shame Continuum

Awkwardness — embarrassment — foolishness — insignificant — disappointment — unwanted — dependency — immaturity — shortcomings — criticised — flawed — devalued — bad — failure — worthlessness — humiliation — faulty — undesirable — dehumanised — degraded — unimportant — irrelevant — imperfect — shame — mortified.

The Jealousy Continuum

Uncertainty — doubt — insecurity — inadequacy — lack — deficiency — failure — faulty — longing — loneliness — resentment — disgust — betrayal — loss – ill-will — distrust — suspicious — unable to be happy for others — possessive — control — disloyalty – inferiority/superiority dichotomy — spite — envy — jealousy.

The Guilt Continuum

Regret — disappointment — worry — fear of not belonging — blame — criticism — remorse — guilt — shame — transgressing morals or values — anxiety — disapproval — sorrow.

The Grief Continuum

Loss — hurt — sadness — sorrow — gloominess — despair — woe — bereavement — grief — inconsolable — distress — lament — sullenness — dejection — desolation — devastation — emptiness — numbness.

The Depression Continuum

Lack of purpose— inability to move on — despair — grief — discouragement — overwhelm — worthlessness — anger — physical, emotional and mental pain — frustration — insecurity — guilt — lack of interest — lack of pleasure — loss — doubt — inability to accept what is happening — inflexibility — lack of direction — sadness — isolation — emptiness — loneliness — mental, emotional and physical exhaustion.

The Trauma Continuum

Isolation — detachment — disassociation — powerless — weak — numb — helpless — vulnerable — scared — fearful — defenceless — unsafe — unprotected — traumatised — hypervigilant — collapse — victimised — frozen — suppression — shock — repression — disturbed — feeling damaged — paralysed — devastation — insecure.

The Powerlessness Continuum

Idleness — laziness — stuck — inaction — sluggishness — torpor — inertia — defenceless — weakness — procrastination — lack — sabotage — resistance — lethargy — powerlessness — helplessness — struggle — hopelessness — scarcity — invisible — suffering.

The Sabotage Continuum

Prostitution (selling yourself out or short) — sacrifice — doing something that is not good for you — giving up something that is good for you — running from your ideal — self-criticism — worthlessness — victimhood — detrimental words, behaviours and actions — criticism — belittling — pretending — procrastinating.

Empowered Tapping® Script

Use the following script to work through the various emotional expressions that limit your ability to create new possibilities. For example, to address bitterness (part of the anger continuum), insert the word 'bitterness' into the script at Round 1 TH and again in Round 2 at the TH, EB, UE, TL, CB and UB points. When you add the relevant emotion from the continuum, adjust the tense of the emotion and the wording. The wording for this example would become:

"Even though it's normal for me to respond to my experiences with bitterness"

Other emotions will have slightly different wording, for example:

"Even though it's normal for me to respond to my experiences by catastrophising"

Or:

"Even though it's normal for me to respond to my experiences by feeling anxious"

As you tap each of your meridian points, say this script aloud.

Emotional Continuum Template Script

Round 1 (Repeat twice)

TH: Even though it's normal for me to respond to my experiences with/by feeling ______________.

EB: It's not normal.

SE: It's just my mind trying to manage the overwhelm and confusion I feel.

UE: This triggers off my fear responses that this is how it is and always will be.

TL: This then sets off a cascade of emotionally painful experiences in my mind's reality.

CH: But it's not how my life really has to be.

CB: It's just my fears running stories from my past.

UB: I don't really need certain conditions to exist for me to effectively manage my emotional responses.

UA: And I don't need specific circumstances to exist for me to effectively manage my emotional responses. I already am effectively managing my emotional responses.

Round 2

TH: By interpreting I respond to my experiences with/by feeling ______________ as being about me I have created a belief that this is how it is and always will be.

EB: That belief that I respond to my experiences with/by feeling ______________ is how it is and always will be then colours my experiences, so it feels like it's all I can do.

SE: But it's not all I can do.

UE: By interpreting I respond to my experiences with/by feeling ______________ as being about me I have created a belief that this is how it is and always will be.

TL: That belief that I respond to my experiences with/by feeling ______________ is how it is and always will be then colours my experiences, so it feels like it's all I can do.

CH: But it's not all I can do.

CB: By interpreting I respond to my experiences with/by feeling ____________ as being about me I have created a belief that this is how it is and always will be.

UB: That belief that I respond to my experiences with/by feeling ____________ is how it is and always will be then colours my experiences, so it feels like it's all I can do.

UA: But it's not all I can do.

Round 3

TH: I'm letting it all go.

EB: I'm letting it all go.

SE: I'm letting it all go.

UE: I'm letting go of all that no longer serves me.

TL: I'm letting it all go.

CH: I'm letting go of all that no longer serves me.

CB: I'm letting it all go.

UB: I'm letting go of all that no longer serves me.

UA: I'm letting it all go.

Round 4

TH: The only truth is I already am effectively managing my emotional responses.

All remaining points: I already am effectively managing my emotional responses.

Acknowledgements

There I was, thinking I was in Tahiti to celebrate birthdays and friendship with my bestie Erin Richardson, and I was, but my brain also did what it does. I'm known to have creative thoughts pop into my head as soon as I have a break, and that's how this book came into being. I am eternally grateful for how I am utilised for the purpose of transforming awareness and bringing new ways of perceiving our experiences into the world, even if sometimes I'd like to be sleeping.

I thank all my friends and clients who not only support but encourage me to write down all my insights and awarenesses to share with the wider world. In particular, I would love to thank Shalla O'Keefe, Maureen Dodson, Atheena Tyris and Erin Richardson for your feedback as I put words to paper. An additional thank you to Erin for eagerly spending our time in Tahiti tapping all the scripts that came to me there.

Thank you, Leela, for your magnificent editing guidance. You have helped bring the intent of this book to life, and I really appreciate all your suggestions and improvements as we went through the editing process.

To Scott and Trudy King, thank you for all your support and faith in my work. It is an absolute joy to work with two authentic souls whose priorities are supporting the best in others through truth and honesty.

Thank you for reading this book. I sincerely hope you are enjoying the shifts in consciousness Empowered Tapping® is affording you.

Acknowledgements

About the Author

Leonie Blackwell is known for her expertise in emotional wellness, having worked in a variety of settings as a teacher, youth worker and naturopath for over four decades. The author of *Making Sense of the Insensible* and *The Box of Inner Secrets*, she also wrote the chapter *Magnetic Joy* in Joe Vitale's book, *The Prosperity Factor*. Leonie is the creator of Empowered Tapping®. Her online school, Bwell Institute, hosts practitioner training courses (Flower Essence Therapy and Empowered Tapping®), the Tappers Tribe, dozens of personal development classes and the Healthy Optimal Wellness (HOW) Community. In 2015, Leonie travelled to Jordan as a member of a pilot project that trained and mentored NGO and UNAWRA workers. This inspirational program assisted refugees in eliminating their symptoms of post-traumatic stress. Leonie has held her Empowered Tapping® Retreat in Ladakh, India.

For further information,
visit www.leonieblackwell.au

Check out the Tappers Tribe:
www.leonieblackwell.au/tappers-tribe

Follow Leonie's Empowered Tapping® on Facebook:
www.facebook.com/empoweredtapping

Notes

Notes

Notes

Notes

Notes

Notes

Notes